LIKE SOMETHING FLYING BACKWARDS

C.D. Wright has published eleven collections of poems in the US, including three book-length poems, *One Big Self* (Twin Palms Publishers, 2003; Copper Canyon Press, 2007), *Deepstep Come Shining* (Copper Canyon Press, 1998) and *Just Whistle* (Kelsey Street Press, 1994). She was State Poet of Rhode Island from 1994 to 1999. On a fellowship for writers for the Wallace Foundation, she curated *The Lost Roads Project: a walk-in book of Arkansas*, an exhibition which toured throughout her native state.

She is also a recipient of fellowships and awards from the Guggenheim Foundation, the National Endowment for the Arts, the Bunting Institute, the Foundation for Contemporary Arts, the Lannan Foundation and the John D. and Catherine T. MacArthur Foundation.

Wright is a member of the faculty of literary arts at Brown University in Providence, Rhode Island. For 30 years she edited Lost Roads Publishers with her husband, poet Forrest Gander.

Like Something Flying Backwards: New & Selected Poems (Bloodaxe Books, 2007), her first UK edition, is expanded from *Steal Away: selected and new poems* (Copper Canyon Press, 2003), a finalist for the Griffin Poetry Prize.

C.D. WRIGHT

Like Something Flying Backwards

NEW & SELECTED POEMS

for Angela

BLOODAXE BOOKS

ISBN: 978 1 85224 762 1

First published 2007 by
Bloodaxe Books Ltd,
Highgreen,
Tarset,
Northumberland NE48 1RP.

www.bloodaxebooks.com
For further information about Bloodaxe titles
please visit our website or write to
the above address for a catalogue.

Bloodaxe Books Ltd acknowledges
the financial assistance of
Arts Council England, North East.

Cover design: Neil Astley & Pamela Robertson-Pearce.
Cover printing: J. Thomson Colour Printers Ltd, Glasgow.

Printed in Great Britain by
Bell & Bain Limited, Glasgow, Scotland.

Acknowledgements

The poems in this selected volume were first published in the UK by Bloodaxe Books in 2007 under licence from Copper Canyon Press. Originally published in the United States in 1998, 2002 and 2005 by Copper Canyon Press.

Like Something Flying Backwards is an expanded edition based on *Steal Away: selected and new poems* (Copper Canyon Press, USA, 2002 & 2003), with the addition of the following: "A Farm Boy" (94-100); complete text of *Deepstep Come Shining* (191-248) instead of the previous selection; final poem from *One Big Self* (266); new poems (267-72 & 279-92); and four poems from *Cooling Time* (273-78).

Translations of the Gospel Back into Tongues was first published by State University of New York Press, 1982, Paul Zweig, Editor, SUNY Poetry Series, Shirley Clay Scott and C.K. Williams, poetry editorial board.

Further Adventures with You was first published by Carnegie-Mellon University Press, 1986, Gerald Costanzo, Editor.

String Light was first published by The University of Georgia Press, 1991, Bin Ramke, Poetry Series Editor.

Just Whistle: a valentine was first published by Kelsey St. Press, 1993, with gratitude to the editorial board, especially Rena Rosenwasser. The Kelsey St. Press edition included photographs by Deborah Luster.

Tremble was first published by The Ecco Press, 1996, Daniel Halpern, Editor.

Deepstep Come Shining was first published by Copper Canyon Press, 1998, Sam Hamill, Editor. With gratitude to Michael Wiegers, Managing Editor.

One Big Self: Prisoners of Louisiana was first published by Twin Palms Publishers, 2003, photographs by Deborah Luster, Jack Woody, Editor. A text edition, *One Big Self: An Investigation* was published by Copper Canyon Press, 2007, Michael Wiegers, Editor.

Steal Away: selected and new poems was published by Copper Canyon Press 2002 and 2003, Sam Hamill, Editor.

Cooling Time: An American Poetry Vigil was first published by Copper Canyon Press in 2005, Sam Hamill, Editor.

Grateful acknowledgment is made to the editors of the following print and web journals in which some of these poems or versions thereof first appeared:

American Letters and Commentary, The American Poetry Review, The Apostle's Bar, Arshile, Black Warrior Review, BRICK, Brown Alumnae Monthly, Caliban,

Chelsea, Colorado Review, Conjunctions, Crossroads: Journal of the Poetry Society of America, Denver Quarterly, Doubletake, Epoch, Fence, Field, Five Fingers Review, Fourteen Hills, Ironwood, Jacket, Julbilat, Kilometer Zero, The New Yorker, NO, Organica, The Paris Review, The Pennsylvania Review, Phoebe, Ploughshares, Poetry East, The Prose Poem, Quarterly West, raccoon, Radcliffe Quarterly, rooms, Slate, Southern Review, Sulfur, Three Rivers Poetry Journal, Torque, TriQuarterly, turnrow, Verse, Volt, The World.

Special thanks to Bradford Morrow for printing the full set of "Retablos" along with their translations, and the photographs by Deborah Luster for which they were composed. Retablos #1, #2, #3 appeared in *Fourteen Hills*. An excerpt from *Just Whistle* also appeared in *Conjunctions #17,* the tenth anniversary issue. The epistolary poems are from *One Big Self: Prisoners of Louisiana,* a project in collaboration with photographer Deborah Luster. They appeared in *Conjunctions #35, American Poetry.* A chapbook from *Deepstep Come Shining* was published in *Black Warrior Review* (Vol. 24, No. 2), Christopher Chambers, Editor, Alan Mays, Poetry Editor. Additional passages from *Deepstep Come Shining* were first published in *Fence,* Rebecca Wolff, Editor.

I would also like to thank the National Endowment for the Arts, the John Simon Guggenheim Memorial Foundation, the Mary Ingraham Bunting Institute at Radcliffe College, the Whiting Foundation, and the Lila Wallace–Reader's Digest Fund for fellowships that were an immense help during the years in which these poems were written. I would also like to thank the Center for Documentary Studies at Duke University for the Dorothea Lange–Paul Taylor Prize for support for a collaboration with photographer Deborah Luster.

I would also like to thank the John D. and Catherine T. MacArthur Foundation for a five-year fellowship the benefits of which I cannot finally estimate.

This original US edition from which this book has been adapted was designed and typeset by Phil Kovacevich. The poems are set in Minion, a font inspired by classical, old style typefaces of the late Renaissance. The titles are set in Orator, a font designed for IBM typewriters by John Scheppler.

CONTENTS

TREMBLE (1996)

THE ROSESUCKER RETABLOS

Rosesucker Retablo #1

Though it be the season   of falling men
Presaged by crop circles
And compact moving masses
Long dresses made all the more dolorous by dark umbrellas
From these very fingers emerge   pistols of love
Lilies of forgiveness
And as you enter the eye   in this palm
Chuparosa   bind me   to your secrecy
Open your munificent purse   hoard me

Retablo del Chuparosa #1

Aunque sea la estación   de los hombres caídos
Presagiada por los círculos del grano
Y las masas compactas en movimiento
Los vestidos largos aún más dolorosos por los paraguas negros
De estos mismos dedos surgen   pistolas de amor
Lirios de perdón
Y conforme entras en el ojo   en esta palma
Chuparosa   átame   a lo que guardas en secreto
Abre tu bolso munífico   abárcame

Rosesucker Retablo #2

And though my birds be torn   to rags of smoke
And I into a nexus   of feather and ash
You must move ahead   unencumbered
By melancholy or defects
Behold the woman   Chuparosa
May you never endure a week
Without letters from an inmate
Never the day without apples or bread
Come in   from distant penetralia   blasted immaculacy

Retablo del Chuparosa #2

Y a pesar de que mis pájaros se vuelvan   jirones de humo
Y yo el nexo   entre la pluma y la ceniza
Debes proseguir   sin el peso de
La melancolía o los defectos
Observa a la mujer   Chuparosa
Que nunca sobrevivas una semana
Sin las cartas de un encarcelado
Nunca el día en que no haya ni manzanas ni pan
Entra   de distantes santuarios   pureza maculada

ROSESUCKER RETABLO #3

With a drink of lasting rain   I may be clean gone
Hasta luego   I troth thee and thine   only ease in childbirth
Only comfort in the dying   only thorns   to whip the legs
Of the insolent daughters
But because they are only roses
There will be so very little pain
For your part   Chuparosa   you must leave
Everything exactly as it is   in order to remain
Unpossessed and unforsaken   all the way to the end

RETABLO DEL CHUPAROSA #3

Con un trago de lluvia perdurable   tal vez me haya esfumado sin mengua
Hasta luego   os doy mi palabra   nada más que sosiego en el parto
Sólo comodidad en la muerte   sólo espinas   para fustigar las piernas
De las hijas insolentes
Pero sólo porque son rosas
Habrá un ínfimo dolor
En cuanto a ti   Chuparosa   debes dejar
Todo exactamente como es   para quedar
Unánime y probo   de aquí hasta el final

traducción de Gabriel Bernal Granados

from TRANSLATIONS OF THE GOSPEL
BACK INTO TONGUES (1982)

ALLA BREVE LOVING

Three people drinking out of the bottle
in the living room.
A cold rain. Quiet as a mirror.

One of the men
stuffs his handkerchief in his coat,
climbs the stairs with the girl.
The other man is left sitting

at the desk with the wine and the headache,
turning an old Ellington side
over in his mind. And over.

He held her like a saxophone
when she was his girl.
Her tongue trembling at the reed.

The man lying next to her now
thinks of another woman.
Her white breath idling

before he drove off.
He said something about a spell,
watching the snow fall on her shoulders.

The musician
crawls back into his horn,
ancient terrapin
at the approach of the wheel.

THE SECRET LIFE OF MUSICAL INSTRUMENTS

Between midnight and Reno
the world borders on a dune.
The bus does not stop.

The boys in the band have their heads on the rest.
They dream like so-and-sos.

The woman smokes
one after another.
She is humming "Strange Fruit."
There is smoke in her clothes, her voice,
but her hair never smells.

She blows white petals off her lapel,
tastes salt.
It is a copacetic moon.

The instruments do not sleep in their dark cribs.
They keep cool, meditate.
They have speech with strangers:

Come all ye faithless
young and crazy victims of love.
Come the lowlife and the highborn
all ye upside-down shitasses.

Bring your own light.
Come in. Be lost. Be still.
If you miss us at home
we'll be on our way to the reckoning.

for Claudia Burson

BENT TONES

There was a dance at the black school.
In the shot houses people were busy.

A woman washed her boy in a basin, sucking
a cube of ice to get the cool.

The sun drove a man in the ground like a stake.
Before his short breath climbed the kitchen's steps

she skipped down the walk in a clean dress.
Bad meat on the counter. In the sky, broken glass.

When the local hit the trestle everything trembled—
the trees she blew out of, the shiver owl,

lights next door. With her fast eye
she could see Little Floyd
changing his shirt for the umpteenth time.

Tours

A girl on the stairs listens to her father
beat up her mother.
Doors bang.
She comes down in her nightgown.

The piano stands there in the dark
like a boy with an orchid.

She plays what she can
then she turns the lamp on.

Her mother's music is spread out
on the floor like brochures.

She hears her father
running through the leaves.

The last black key
she presses stays down, makes no sound,
someone putting their tongue where their tooth had been.

BLAZES

A man came home with my brothers.
He had on a hunting vest,
a bird losing blood and feathers from the pouch.

I thought of a burning bush.

It was raining again,
someone driving nails in a board.

I brushed the folds out of the tablecloth.
The visitor stood in the steam
lifting off the table.
He wiped his hands on my apron.

The voice of my father came on
gentle as a lamp
a page being turned in its light.

They pushed their plate away, took their chair to the front room,
and lit up. I went to mine.
It was a school night. I held my pillow to my chest
and said Kiss me Frankie.

I was old enough
to know love is blind as the old woman
pulled down the hall by her dog.

Their guns leaned against the wall
but men in those days kept themselves armed
in the dark and rain.

It never stopped.
Everyone who could handle an oar
headed for hell in a boat.

I thought of a burning bush.

LIBRETTO

Night is dark
on the streets without names.

Men piss in the ditch, on the toe of their shoes
thinking it must be rain or hail.

The feet of their women swell like a melon.
Their ironing boards bow
under the weight of beautiful linen
they do for other women.

Radios are turned up to beat thunder,
translations of the gospel
back into tongues.

The tiger lilies' tremble.
Bottles busted, somebody cut.

A man in a black shirt
gets off the bus with no suitcase,
leans on his wife. Umbrella
with a broken spoke.

A girl sits out-of-doors in her slip.
She turns fourteen, twenty-eight, fifty-six,
goes crazy.

The saxophone plays it for somebody else.
Play hell.

CLOCKMAKER WITH BAD EYES

I close the shop at six. Welcome wind,
weekend with two suns, night with a travel book,
the dog-eared sheets of a bed
I will not see again.

I not of time, lost in time
learned from watches—
a second is a killing thing.

Live your life. Your eyes go. Take your body
out for walks along the waters
of a cold and loco planet.

Love whatever flows. Cooking smoke, woman's blood,
tears. Do you hear what I'm telling you?

Obedience of the Corpse

The midwife puts a rag in the dead woman's hand,
takes the hairpins out.

She smells apples,
wonders where she keeps them in the house.
Nothing is under the sink
but a broken sack of potatoes growing eyes.

She hopes the mother's milk is good awhile longer,
the woman up the road is still nursing.
She remembers the neighbor
and the dead woman never got along.

A limb breaks.
She knows it's not the wind.
Somebody needs to set out some poison.

She looks to see if the woman wrote down any names,
finds a white shirt to wrap the baby in.
It's beautiful she thinks—
snow nobody has walked on.

THE NIGHT BEFORE THE SENTENCE
IS CARRIED OUT

                  a woman is riding a bus
with a sack of black apples in her lap.

The bus stalls on the dam.
She pulls a knife out of the sack, throws it
in the water with the blade half open

like the eyes of a lawyer
who has been drinking heavy
for a month. More than a month.

He passes out in his boat.
When he comes to, the lake is another man's
suit, in the billfold
photo of another man's wife.

The woman waits for everyone to get off
before she does.
She reaches up to put the pins in her hair.

The condemned man is rubbing his arms
thinking about someone
he used to be married to.
He reaches under the cot, touches the cold wire.

She stands up brushing her clothes,
the bottom falls out of the sack.
She leaves the apples scattered in the aisle.

Vanish

Because I did not die
I sit in the captain's chair
going deaf in one ear, blind in the other.
I live because the sea does.

All I remember, three stories
of rooms:

In one, a girl is sewing a dress
for her brother's funeral.
Jars of rhubarb cool on the porch.
A man puts his music away,
but not the instrument.
The spare room is made up,
the guest wants a lift into town.

A light stumbles in the corridor—
someone who doesn't know where to go
when the bar shuts down for blue laws.

Steal away,
shadows of old boyfriends.

Since that night
some of us have looked for better lamps
to read by.
Others have worn a soft robe,
stirred the coals.

Because I did not marry
I wash by the light of the body.
Soap floats out of my mind.
I have almost forgotten
the sailor whose name I did not catch,
wave on a shell, his salty tongue on an ear.

WANDERER IN HIS THIRTIETH YEAR

Clearly, the stores were closed.
The road open.
Snow blowing up the steps
like dust. I let him in,
took his things.
He just wanted to sit
in the dark, watch the fire.
He did not drink
so much as he slept.
Not sleep
so much as he dreamed.
He left before I got up.
The longhair bore her litter
on the fleece of his coat.
One bus groaned
over the mountain.
Carrying one rider.
Snow whirling over the floor.

THE HANDFISHING RETABLOS

HANDFISHING RETABLO #1

Leftover shoofly pie   charred baby bed
Stuffed bear   in the raked dirt
Smoke coming out of its butt   snake eyes
In the robin nest   piano repossessed   who decides
Who sits down   to pee   who stands in the mist   if
There is something   worth knowing   if
There is some one thing   important for us
To know   we come   to build worlds   arriba los corazones
Media Naranja   pray keep us   in contact with our ground

RETABLO DE LA PESCA MANUAL #1

Sobras de un merengue   cuna carbonizada
Osito de peluche   en la mugre apelmazada
Humo que sale de sus nalgas   ojos de serpiente
En el nido del petirrojo   piano embargado   quien decide
Quien se sienta   a orinar   quien se para en la bruma   si
Hay algo   digno de saberse   si
Hay alguna cosa   que valga la pena
Saber   llegamos   a construir mundos   arriba los corazones
Media Naranja   favor de dejarnos   en contacto con tu suelo

Handfishing Retablo #2

Followed us   to the shaft   end of the song   Qué milagro
At the nock end   your flight   at the point   your breath
The worst man   a stone   the worst woman
A mill   the hair Chuparosa the hair   always gets caught
Leaf on leaf   worm by worm   we museum   in a box
On the other side   of the clearing   is another
Forest   fraught with unknowns   O my flammable
Pajamas   O my degenerating fibroids
When they lift the prints off our breasts   will they be yours
Young epitaph   kiss me   then count your teeth

Retablo de la pesca manual #2

Nos siguieron   hasta el pozo   final de la canción   Qué milagro
Al trunco final   de nuestro vuelo   al momento que   tu respiración
El peor de los hombres   una piedra   la peor de las mujeres
Un molino   el cabello Chuparosa el cabello   siempre se enreda
Hoja sobre hoja   gusano tras gusano   los atesoramos   en una caja
Al otro lado   del claro   hay otro
Bosque   repleto de incógnitas   O mi pijama
Inflamable   O mis fibroides en descomposición
Cuando revoquen las huellas de nuestro senos   serán tuyos
Joven epitafio   bésame   luego cuéntate los dientes

HANDFISHING RETABLO #3

Walking   from a corona of bees   Carumba
Our mind sees   him walking   on our color monitor
For too long   have we been   trying too hard
Carumba   dreaming   too little   were it not
So far down   we love but   no lock   can keep him
In house   discalced   he walks   El Camino Real
Through smoking rubble   given the choice   of eyebrows
Or scales   which would it be   Carumba   you're asking me
Were it not   so far down   plug of poetry in jaw
He is a step ahead   all ear and reverie   way old way down

RETABLO DE LA PESCA MANUAL #3

Viene   de una corona de abejas   Carumba
Nuestras mentes lo   ven caminando   en un monitor de color
Hemos heco   demasiado tiempo   el esfuerzo
Carumba   hemos soñado   muy poco   si no fuera
Demasiado lejos   amamos mas   ninguna llave   puede retenerlo
En casa   camina   descalzo   El Camino Real
Por los restos humeantes   habiendo elegido   entre cejas
O escalas   cuál podría ser   Carumba   me preguntas que
Si no fuera   demasiado lejos   la clavija de la poesía en la quijada
Él está un paso al frente   de todo oído y todo ensueño
                sendero viejo sendero abajo

Handfishing Retablo #4

Born not stillborn   one elderly baby
At the bedstead of mourning   below depot town
Half god half hart   hodfuls of blood   dirt daubers in the dreadlocks
Potter wasps you say   in the red zone   where it isn't illegal to serve
An egg   sunny-side up   now listen   Chuparosa
He's had it   this baby's had it   with that old tired bullshit
Whether or not the danger is past   everready   unscripted   unbred
To become a memory   free air   we serve   *Laissez*
Le bon temps roulez   help your selves   flywheels turned *ici*

Retablo de la pesca manual #4

Nacido no nonato   un bebé longevo
En la cama desnuda del duelo   bajo el pueblo-almacén
Mitad dios mitad venado   coágulos de sangre   cerdas sucias en las trenzas
Avispas de barro dices   en el mercado negro   donde no es ilegal servir
Un huevo   estrellado   ahora escucha   Chuparosa
Ya se hartó   este bebé ya se hartó   de esta misma mierda trasnochada
Haya o no pasado el peligro   infalible   no escrito   descastado
De convertirse así en un recuerdo   aire libre   servimos   *Laissez*
Le bon temps roulez   ayúdense a sí mismos   los volantes vueltos *ici*

traducción de Gabriel Bernal Granados

from FURTHER ADVENTURES
WITH YOU (1986)

WAGES OF LOVE

The house is watched, the watchers only planets.

Very near the lilac
                   a woman leaves her night soil
to be stepped in. Like other animals.
                   Steam lifts off her mess.

They have power, but not water.
                   Pregnant. She must be.

The world is all that is the case.

You can hear the strike of the broom, a fan
                   slicing overhead light.
At the table the woman stares at a dish
                   of peaches, plums; black ants
filing down the sill to bear away the fly.

Everywhere in America is summer. The young
                   unaware they are young, their minds
on other wounds or the new music.

The heart some bruised fruit
knocked loose by a long stick
                   aches at the stem.
It's not forbidden to fall out of love
                   like from a tree.

As for the tenants whose waters
                   will break in this bed,
May they live through the great pain;
may their offspring change everything—

                   because everything must change.

The man joins the woman in the kitchen. They touch
                   the soft place of their fruit.
They enter in, tell their side, and pass through.

PROVINCES

Where the old trees reign with their forward dark
light stares through a hole in the body's long
house. The bed rolls away from the body,
and the body is forced to find a chair. At some hour
the body sequesters itself in a shuttered room
with no clock. When a clean sheet of paper floats by,
the head inclines on its axis. It is one of those
common bodies that felt it could not exist without loving,
but has in fact gone on and on without love.
Like a cave that has stopped growing, we don't call it dead,
but dormant. Now the body is on all fours, one arm
engaged in pulling hair from a trap, an activity
the body loathes. When the time comes, the body
feeds on marinated meats and fruits trained to be luscious.
Once the body had ambitions—to be tall and remain
soft. No more, but it enjoys rappelling to the water.
Because the body's dwelling is stone, perched over water,
we say the body is privileged. Akin to characters
in Lawrence books, its livelihood is obscured. It owns
a horse named Campaign it mounts on foggy morns.
That was the body's first lie. It has no horse
and wouldn't climb on one. Because the body lives
so far from others, it likes reading about checkered lives
in the metrópoli. It likes moving around at night under its dress.
When it travels, bottles of lotion open in its bags.
Early in March the big rains came—washing all good thoughts
from the body's cracks and chinks. By now the body admits
it is getting on, and yet, continues to be tormented
by things being the way they are. Recently the body took
one of the old trees for a wife, but the union has broken down.
The light has bored out of the body's long house.
Fog envelops its stone flanks. Still the body
enjoys rappelling to the water. And it likes the twenty-four-hour stores,
walking up and down the aisles, not putting a thing in its basket.

TREATMENT

This is a 16-mm film of seven minutes in which no words are spoken. But for a few hand-tinted elements—the girl's dress, the sax, sky at church—the color is black-and-white. The camera reports in the all-knowing third except in handheld shots when it momentarily exposes the driver's field of vision.

The bus rocks out of ruts and over creek rocks at predawn. The driver hasn't picked up any children. He has the radio on and a cigarette lit. Isn't paying attention to either. His headlights scan the road, and webs in the trees, as if they were searchlights. His mind is bent, as his posture and his face reveal. A girl dresses in purple in the dark. She feels along the wallpaper to the kitchen, fixes oatmeal, warms coffee to which she adds globs of honey. She makes a sandwich for lunch. She starts to eat out of the pot on the stove. Stops and gets a bowl from a high cabinet and sits at the table. She taps with her foot to a tune she hums only inside herself. When she goes back upstairs to comb her hair and make an irregular part, to tinkle—she hears her parents. Their bedsprings. A shot of them under many covers. Apparently her mother has told her she is a love child. She understands, so her listening isn't upsetting. She steals in her younger brother's room and leaves a bird she had folded from one sheet of paper on the nightstand. When she hears the bus shifting at the foot of the hill she grabs sweater and tablet and flies past the lunchsack on the banister. Their house isn't beautiful but its shadows are. The driver greets her with Hey Princess. That look. She sits close to the rear. The driver climbs the hill and puts it in neutral under an elm stand. He jerks the handbrake. The camera is in back and shooting forward as he comes down the aisle—it is behind her. He looms larger than he is and walks as if the bus were in motion. The rape is explicit. The camera shoots out the back and side windows every few seconds to see if anyone, another vehicle, approaches. There are no more shots of the girl. The parents' house is shown from the yard and from the foot of her window. Light breaks in the trees, a cool sun. You hear the bus grind, the children, as the bus fills and proceeds. Then a field of high grass, a white church. No roads leading there. No cars parked nearby. Slight quality of a different world. A saxophone is played. A full choir accompanies. A silent congregation: all stand, motionless. All adults. Pharoah Sanders stands in front of the choir stall in white robes. He plays with his eyes shut. He plays a curved soprano. His foot taps to an interior beat. Clearly he's an Angel. With the horn he lures. Accuses. His solo has a timeless aura. The doors of the church blow open. The driver falls onto the aisle. He begins to squirm on his belly toward the Pharoah. It is a long journey. The Pharoah wails controllably. The choir sways, claps; the congregation keeps quiet, light breaks in the trees and indistinct voices of many children fill the nave as if they were boarding a bus.

THE CINEMATOGRAPHER'S FÅRÖ ISLAND LOG

Like so many stories this begins
with a house harbored under larch;
a bag of green tea dropped over the rim
of a handed-down cup.

It begins with the pale husband, limited light;
fingers parting the labia
and her ear in his mouth.

Soon, the man is downstairs with a towel,
the peripatetic camera at his heels.

They will dress in darkness for work,
him going without shoes in the house, habit
from the Japanese girl he loved first.

He stares at the lake carved like a mirror
and listens to the sough of her comb—

The camera studies the venation of new leaves
on a lightning-split tree near shore.

The tea is greener now and cold.
The woman he married is seated
before the mirror. She stares
through concentric circles in the glass

and asks of the figure leaving
the shadowy cove of their hall,
What is your favorite body of water. And why.

HOTELS

In the semidark we take everything off,
love standing, inaudible; then we crawl into bed.
You sleep with your head balled up in its dreams,
I get up and sit in the chair with a warm beer,
the lamp off. Looking down on a forested town
in a snowfall I feel like a novel—dense
and vivid, uncertain of the end—watching
the bundled outlines of another woman another man
hurrying toward the theater's blue tubes of light.

ELEMENTS OF NIGHT

Cold food, homework, and hair. Rooms with a radiator and no books.
Moths like flour. Venetian blinds. Wallets tossed from cars. Cockeye.
Fish do not slow down. A good robe. Pencils. The back of his head.
Breeze. Scene in another language. Beds hard as boards. A girl climbing
a fence like a vine. Records left out of covers. Moving furniture. Cleaning
women. Clocks. A praying mantis in a jar. Barns blown down. Her rainy
underarms. Faith hope and hypocrisy. Trees growing old. Boats in fields.
Guests. A box on fire. Icetrays. Ironing. Genitals like underwater fruit.
People drinking out of a bottle. Urine. Crimes of passion. Mascara. Valet
parking. A small college green. Adjustable lamp. *Even the way she holds
her neck.* Trailers. Slamming doors. Fine rugs, baby grand. Change
for the phone. A podalic version. Jobs taken on the lam. Radar.
A bad mole. Unpublished number. Houses you can't see from the road.
Television. The glory hole. Now that visiting hours are over.
Musicians on break. A novel like a neighbor. Vestibules of mirrors
and light. Sprayed on a wall: Leo dies alone. Also: 1981, Where is
my beautiful daughter.

LAPSE

After the last war we drafted pages and pages
of our final will and testimony. Then we set off
in a different direction. What we left behind
didn't amount to much. I was all for living
the fictitious life. We chipped in to drive
until we ran out of gas. We wound up in one lost valley.
Cold cash passed through us like lightning through trees.
We nearly died laughing. We weren't drunk.
Winter was mild, the spring came in torrents.
Under the duck cloth with handkerchiefs on our heads—
due to a hat shortage—there was talk of building
a spur back to the main highway. Our jokes
wore thin, our jeans. We printed a paper
by night, the single issue being peace.
Water oaks in the carlights looked like I don't know what.
We slept fine. The cooking wasn't bad.
The part I remember fondly—him,
sitting up in the seminaked sunshine,
                           his hair blowing all around.

SCRATCH MUSIC

How many threads have I broken with my teeth. How many times
have I looked at the stars and felt ill. Time here is divided into before
and since your shuttering in 1978. I remember hanging on to the
hood of the big-fendered Olds with a mess of money in my purse.
Call that romance. Some memory precedes you: when I wanted
lederhosen because I'd read *Heidi*. And how I wanted my folks to
build a fallout shelter so I could arrange the cans. And coveting
Mother's muskrat. I remember college. And being in Vista: I asked
the librarian in Banks, the state's tomato capital, if she had any black
literature and she said they used to have *Little Black Sambo* but the white
children tore out pages and wrote ugly words inside. Someone said
if I didn't like Banks I should go to Moscow. I said, Come on, let's go
outside and shoot the hoop. I've got a jones to beat your butt. I haven't
changed. Now if I think of the earth's origins, I get vertigo. When I
think of its death, I fall. I've picked up a few things. I know if you
want songbirds, plant berry trees. If you don't want birds, buy a
rubber snake. I remember that town with the Alcoa plant I toured.
The manager kept referring to the workers as Alcoans. I thought of
hundreds of flexible metal beings bent over assemblages. They
sparked. What would I do in Moscow. I have these dreams—relatives
loom over my bed. We should put her to sleep, Lonnie says. Go home
old girl, go home, my aunt says. Why should I go home before her I
want to say. But I am bereft. So how is life in the other world. Do
you get the news. Are you allowed a pet. But I wanted to show you
how I've grown, what I know: I keep my bees far from the stable,
they can't stand how horses smell. And I know sooner or later an old
house will need a new roof. And more than six years have whistled
by since you blew your heart out like the porchlight. Reason and
meaning don't step into another lit spot like a well-meaning stranger
with a hat. And mother's mother, who has lived in the same house
ten-times-six years, told me, We didn't know we had termites until
they swarmed. Then we had to pull up the whole floor. "Too late, no
more…," you know the poem. But you, you bastard. You picked up a
gun in winter as if it were a hat and you were leaving a restaurant:
full, weary, and thankful to be spending the evening with no one.

ILLUMINATIONS

I have heard of one man of atonement:
in a tent on a frozen lake
under the aurora australis, he sleeps
in his down, dreaming of no one,
his airplane. There is the oil
he guards with his body. The lamp
at his back like another body.
A gloved finger rubs a blue eyelid.
There is horror first of the life
that goes on below ice. By degrees
the limbs harden with light. Thinking
of a word no longer spoken by men:
                              vouchsafe.

THIS COUPLE

Now is when we love to sit before mirrors
with a dark beer or hand out leaflets
at chain-link gates or come together after work
listening to each other's hard day. The engine dies,
no one hurried to go in. We might
walk around in the yard not making a plan.
The freeway is heard but there's no stopping
progress, and the week has barely begun. Then
we are dressed. It rains. Our heads rest
against the elevator wall inhaling a stranger;
we think of cliffs we went off
with our laughing friends. The faces
we put our lips to. Our wonderful sex
under whatever we wear. And of the car
burning on the side of the highway. Jukeboxes
we fed. Quarters circulating with our prints.
Things we sent away for. Long drives. The rain. Cafés
where we ate late and once only. Eyes of an animal
in the headlamps. The guestbooks that verify
our whereabouts. Your apple core in the ashtray.
The pay toilets where we sat without paper. Rain.
Articles left with ex-lovers. The famous
ravine of childhood. Movie lines we've stood in
when it really came down. Moments
we have felt forsaken waiting for the others
to step from the wrought-iron compartment,
or passing through some town with the dial
on a Mexican station, wondering for the life of us,
where are we going and when would we meet.

PETITION FOR REPLENISHMENT

We do not mean to complain. We know how it is.
In older, even sadder cultures the worst possible sorts
have been playing hot and cold with people's lives
for much longer. Like Perrow says,
We'll all have baboon hearts one of these days.
We wintered with ample fuel and real tomatoes.
We were allowed to roam, sniffing and chewing
at the tufted crust. We were let to breathe.
That is, we respirated. Now the soft clocks
have gorged themselves on our time. Yet
as our hair blanches and comes out
in hanks, we can tell it is nearly spring—
the students shed their black coats
on the green; we begin to see shade.
Lo, this is the breastbone's embraceable light.
We are here. Still breathing and constellated.

Two Hearts in a Forest

Evening Shade

I am over here, by the tomato cages
gently touching the wire,
watching one lightning bug light another
freshly fucked and childless
an astonished woman in a wedding gown
who can see in the dark, almost.

Lush Life

I could have gone to Stringtown
O I could have wasted away
moaning in the swamped bed
among winged roaches and twisted figs
between the fern and dark thighs.

Hotel Philharmonic

We have arrived drunk, jobless,
brilliant with love.
Music commences:
You hold out your glass
I lift my dress. My hands
saved like candles for a storm
in yours. We fall
through the night's caesura.

Lost Roads

As though following a series of clues, we drove
through this ragged range, a town of magnetic springs
our arms in the window, browning.
The sun was torching the hair of maples.
You didn't sing in key, you sang
"Famous Blue Raincoat."
I had a dream, Life isn't real.
Already the sad rapture entering.

Mountain Herald

This time, the Celebrant vowed, no one would intinct,
blowing the unsteady flames of our face.
We rose and married well, my nose
in your tender swarthiness. I'll never forget
the whirling floor, the bassman's royal head.
As for the uninvited they were asked in.
Melon, not cake, was served;
there was japonica and spirea. Still
they were a little late for the forsythia.
God yes, the forsythia, the forsythia.

FURTHER ADVENTURES WITH YOU

We are on a primeval river in a reptilian den.

There are birds you don't want to tangle with, trees
                    you cannot identify…

                    Somehow we spend the evening with Mingus
in a White Castle. Or somewhere. Nearly drunk. He says
                    he would like to play for the gang.

                    All of us ride to Grandmother Wright's house
in a van. It's her old neighborhood. I think we look
like a carton of colas sitting up stiffly
                    behind the glass.

                    She is recently dead. Some of her belongings
are gone. Her feather mattress has been rolled back
from the springs. It turns out Mingus has forgotten
his cello. We lay on our sides in jackets and jeans
                    as if it were a beach in fall.

                    Then it is Other Mama's house. She is
recently dead. We stretch out on Other Mama's carpet
                    pulling at its nap.

You and I have stomped into A-Mart to buy papers
and schnapps. Two boys, one pimply, the other clear-skinned,
                    blow in with blue handkerchiefs
and a gun. Blue is the one color I notice tonight.
                    They tell us, Take off.

We're gone. We're on the back of the bus with the liquor.
                    The silly boys have shot the package-store clerk.
We're the only suspects. You have a record so you're in a sweat.
You're flashing black, white. Around the nose and mouth

                    you remind me a little of Sam Cooke. I think
he was shot in a motel. A case of sexual madness. We get off
                    at an old bar that shares a wall with a school for girls.

The police collar us there. They separate us for questioning.
                    You show a work card that claims you're a male dancer.
You pull out a gun. Where did you get that. And you blast them.
                    It's their hearts, I think, My God.

You yell out a nonword and hit the doors. I run
through the back. It's the girls school. They seem to be
                    getting ready for a revue. I try to blend in—hoist a mattress,
somebody's music up a staircase. There are racks
                    of costumes on wheels, flats of moving scenery…

There is the river, the horrible featherless bird. The tree,
                    not a true palm but of the palm family.

THE FLOATING LADY RETABLOS

FLOATING LADY RETABLO #1

Remember I remember   I lay my young bullocks
On thine altar   bald and cold as the truth   I was your
Personal all purpose all weather fuck machine   before the finger
Of suspicion could fire one bad shot   the door
Closed on us   I am the emancipated white man   in the paddock
Common as dirt   I scare the horses   I can lie
At any speed   Recuérdame   as I dig you from the short stob
Of memory in my path   Love Letter #3   recuérdame
Siempre   go try your luck on the mountain   if it pleases ye

RETABLO DE LA MUJER FLOTANTE #1

Recuerdo y recuerdo   ofrezco a mis bueyes
En vuestro altar   desnudo y frío como la verdad   yo era tu
Máquina de coger siempre dispuesta   antes que el dedo
De la sospecha pudiera errar el disparo   se nos cerró
La puerta   soy el hombre blanco emancipado   en la dehesa
Común como la mugre   ahuyento a los caballos   puedo mentir
A cualquier velocidad   Recuérdame   as I dig you from the short stob
De la memoria en mi camino   Carta de Amor #3   recuérdame
Siempre   ve a probar suerte en la montaña   si te place

FLOATING LADY RETABLO #2

Unable to read   garden by the moon
Unable to dream   sleep with elvers
The locusts start chewing   the sheets off the line
The big top burns down to the ground   Escúchame
Chuparosa   we begin to see   the typewriting
On the wall   you teach English   in a Vulcan Tool Truck
Rattling full tilt   which is it   what shall be
The remedy   or   what shall the remedy be
Vamanos Chuparosa   we will be the stars' ashtray

RETABLO DE LA MUJER FLOTANTE #2

Incapaz de leer   jardín bajo la luna
Incapaz de soñar   dormida con angulas
Las langostas comienzan a mascar   las sábanas mojadas
El circo se desploma envuelto en llamas   Escúchame
Chuparosa   empezamos a ver   la mecanógrafía
En la pared   das clase de inglés   in a Vulcan Tool Truck
Que traquetea vertiginosamente   cuál es   cuál será
El remedio   o   cuál será el remedio
Vamanos Chuparosa   seremos el cenicero de las estrellas

FLOATING LADY RETABLO #3

This is the shape of the sound   all the information you need
Comes with the light   which melts away   odd   how
Some of the letters   of a life   get printed backwards   how
One pupil looks   for solace   while the other is sweeping the ground
For trouble   how your skin is sensitive as a snail   easy baby
That's my electric eye   it can open anything   from ketchup
To old trousseaux   the Venetian eye I saved for you   easy
Baby   I must disabuse you   of your whiny bugaboos   your
Churlish defenses   from here to yonder baby   it's zero visibility

RETABLO DE LA MUJER FLOTANTE #3

Ésta es la forma del sonido   toda la información que necesitas
Viene con la luz   que se disuelve a la distancia   curioso   cómo
Algunas de las cartas   de una vida   se imprimen al revés   cómo
Un discípulo anda en busca   de solaz   mientras que el otro
    anda barriendo el piso
En busca de problemas   cómo tu piel es sensible como un caracol
    suavecito nene
Ése es mi ojo eléctrico   puede abrir cualquier cosa   desde la catsup
Hasta los viejos *trousseaux*   el ojo veneciano que te guardé   suavecito
Nene   debo quitarte la venda   de tus ridículos fantasmas   tus
Endebles defensas   de acá hasta allá nene   visibilidad: cero

traducción de Gabriel Bernal Granados

from S T R I N G L I G H T (1991)

KING'S DAUGHTERS, HOME FOR UNWED MOTHERS, 1948

Somewhere there figures a man. In uniform. He's not white. He
could be AWOL. Sitting on a mattress riddled with cigarette burns.
Night of a big game in the capital. Big snow.
Beyond Pearl River past Petal and Leaf River and Macedonia;
it is a three-storied house. The only hill around. White.
The house and hill are white. Lighted upstairs, down.
She is up on her elbows, bangs wet in her eyes. The head
of the unborn is visible at the opening. The head
crowns. Many helping hands are on her. She is told not to push.
But breathe. A firm voice. With helping hands.
They open the howl of her love. Out of her issues:

Volumes of letters, morning glories on a string trellis, the job at the
Maybelline factory, the job at the weapons plant, the hummingbird
hive, her hollyhocks, her grandmother's rigid back next to her
grandfather's bow, the briefest reflection of her mother's braid,
her atomizers and silver-backed brush and comb, the steel balls
under her father's knuckles, the moon's punched-out face,
his two-dollar neckties, the peacock coming down the drive; there was
the boy shuffling her way with the melon on his shoulder, car dust all
over his light clothes, the Black Cat fireworks sign on the barn, her
father's death from moving the barn by himself, the family sitting in the
darkened room drinking ice tea after the funeral, tires blown out on the
macadam, the women beaten like eggs, the store with foundation
garments, and boys pelting the girls with peony buds, the meatgrinder
cringing in the corner store, the old icebox she couldn't fix and
couldn't sell so buried to keep out the kids, her grandmother's pride, the
prettiest lavaliere, the pole houses; there was the boy with the melon
shifted to the other shoulder, coming her way, grown taller and darker,
wiping his sweat with his hand, his beautiful Nubian head, older and set
upon by the longingly necked girls from the bottoms, his fishing hole,
learning the equations of equality: six for the white man and none for
the rest; the sloping shadows and blue hollows behind his shack, what
the sunflowers saw, the wide skirts she wore, the lizards they caught, the
eagerness with which they went through each other's folds of hair and
skin, the boy's outnumbered pride...

This couldn't go on, the difficulty of concealment, putting makeup
over a passion mark. 1947, summer of whiskey and victory and
fear. It was long, then over. The letters burned. She heaves. Bleeds.
The infant's head is huge. She tears. He's white. He'll make it
just fine. The firm voice. The hands that helped.
What would become of this boychild. The uniformed man and she
will never know. That they will outlive him. They will never know.
Whether he will do things they never dreamed.

MORE BLUES AND THE ABSTRACT TRUTH

I back the car over a soft, large object;
hair appears on my chest in dreams.
The paperboy comes to collect
with a pit bull. Call Grandmother
and she says, Well you know
death is death and none other.

In the mornings we're in the dark;
even at the end of June
the zucchini keep on the sill.
Ring Grandmother for advice
and she says, O you know
I used to grow so many things.

Then there's the frequent bleeding,
the tender nipples, and the rot
under the floormat. If I'm not seeing
a cold-eyed doctor it is
another gouging mechanic.
Grandmother says, Thanks to the blue rugs
and Eileen Briscoe's elms
the house keeps cool.

Well. Then. You say Grandmother
let me just ask you this:
How does a body rise up again and rinse
her mouth from the tap. And how
does a body put in a plum tree
or lie again on top of another body
or string a trellis. Or go on drying
the flatware. Fix rainbow trout. Grout the tile.
Buy a bag of onions. Beat an egg stiff. Yes,
how does the cat continue
to lick itself from toenail to tailhole.
And how does a body break
bread with the word when the word
has broken. Again. And. Again.
With the wine. And the loaf.

And the excellent glass
of the body. And she says,
Even. If. The. Sky. Is. Falling.
My. Peace. Rose. Is. In. Bloom.

Remarks on Color

1. highway patched with blacktop, service station at the crossroads
2. cream soda in the popbox, man sitting on the popbox
3. a fully grown man
4. filthy toilets, just hold it a little while longer
5. shacks ringed with day lilies, then a columned house in shade
6. condensation off soybeans
7. someone known as Skeeter
8. his whole life
9. flatbed loaded with striped melons
10. Lopez's white car at JB's mother's house
11. katydids crepitating in the tall grass
12. gar wrapping itself in your line
13. gourds strung between poles
14. imagine a tribe of color-blind people, and there could easily be one,
    they would not have the same color concepts as we do
15. that's trumpet vine; that's what we call potato vine
16. no potatoes come of it though
17. no potatoes I know
18. I come back here about three years ago to see if I could eke out a
    living then I run on to Rhonda
19. help me Rhonda help help me Rhonda
20. E-Z on E-Z off
21. out of wedlock, wedlocked
22. planks nailed across kitchen doorway for a bar; living room turned
    into dance floor
23. drinking canned heat
24. the shit can make you permanently blind
25. sizzling nights
26. what do you suppose became of Fontella Bass
27. get your own sound then notes go with your sound—it's like a color,
    my color—I'm black brown with a little red-orange in my skin
28. red looks good on me
29. and yet we could imagine circumstances under which we would say, these
    people see other colors in addition to ours
30. what the Swede concluded: if you want to know what's the matter with blacks
    in America study the other side of the color line
31. I am just telling you what the man figured out

32. there is, after all, no commonly accepted criterion for what is a
     color unless it is one of our colors
33. check this:
34. at the time of his death Presley's was the second most reproduced
     image in the world
35. the first was Mickey Mouse
36. Lansky Brothers—down on Beale—outfitted the johns of Memphis
37. and Elvis
38. R-U ready for Jesus R-U packed up
39. just don't compare me to any white musicians
40. take me witcha man when you go

THE NIGHT I MET LITTLE FLOYD

a Friday or he would not have come to town—he would have
been working in the hills—Esmerelda and the cowboys let Jessie
and me off in front of the duplex—where I lived with
Sonnyman—Little Floyd was in my front room with a book in
his lap—coming back from Tulsa—I did the driving—stripping
gears—we lurched forward—Little Floyd rocked back and
forth in my chair—under the three-way lamp—in Tulsa Jessie
had an abortion—she lay in a coil on the lining of her coat—the
truck groaned on—we stopped for Chinese food—I insisted we
stop—eat—while we were in Tulsa—Jessie was cold—didn't
want to be in a booth—eating Chinese food under fluorescent
tubing—after her abortion—she wanted to go home to her own
hot-water bottle—feel warmer—smaller—looked-after—the
way in church her grandmother's hand used to pet her
incredible hair—offer her half a stick of chewing gum to
quieten her—while the pastor raised Cain—Little Floyd was
big—full-bearded—once in a while he crossed or uncrossed his
sockfeet—a big man reading in a little pool of light—his
hillbilly face absorbed—Jessie cold—in my rocking chair under
the three-way lamp—in the duplex—the truck broke down—
Jessie and I left it hulking beside the road in the brown grass—
under Oklahoma's brown sky—banged the doors and walked—
Little Floyd was Sonnyman's friend—it wasn't long before a
fast loud car came along—skidding to a stop—we squalled
off—with Esmerelda—blasted—and her lapdog—perpetually
runny-eyed—she was going to Arkansas—just one short stop to
make—a farm—not a bit out of the way—to see her
boyfriends—pretty albino boys with albino ponytails—both so
good—not to mention their undulant fields of alfalfa—dense
woods of marijuana—she could not choose—I don't know
another thing about people in Oklahoma—we waited around
for them to cross the line into Arkansas—for the big Friday-
night drunk—which is the real reason Little Floyd was in
town—but he got sidetracked by a book—Sonnyman loaned
him a key—this had to be a Friday—Jessie coiled up in her
cold—Sonnyman gone—the cat rubbing Little Floyd's
sockfeet—in the brothers' farmhouse—a despondent couch—

three lame chairs—stereo—a no-good television—woodstove—
everyone but Jessie standing by the oven—smoking—
blasted—she wanted to be home—be warmer—smaller—
looked-after—at last one brother picked up his hat—we were
close to the line—Esmerelda and the cowboys let us off in front
of the duplex—we could see through the Visqueen—the man
rocking in the lighted room—a book in his lap—the cat
arranging herself across the fly of his jeans—Sonny's friend—
reading *Ladies from Hell*—in two years Sonnyman would be
dead—in a few more years Jessie's boyfriend died too—the
truck belonged to him—Little Floyd keeps coming in from the
hills on Friday—closes the bar—if I leave the key in the spider
plant he falls out on the floor—snores until late on Saturday—
takes me out to breakfast—Jessie moved—she fell into a dark
shaft of money—married a sweet East Texas man—the truck
remained on the side of the road a week or so—Jessie's landlord
crossed the line into Oklahoma with chains—and dragged its
chassis back to Arkansas—maybe we didn't have enough good
times—not enough times when someone jumped up and said—
let's float the Buffalo—take off for the river with a borrowed
canoe—come back the next evening—dirty dishes still on the
table—we tended to wait around until we were left by the
hellbent whiskered men with their indelible smells—our sorry
shoes huddled together by the bed—Oklahoma was a stand of
trees without leaves—brown grass brown sky—weathervanes
sharp and thin as women blown this way and that—cold beef
suppers—3.2 beer—Arkansas—a pot of lentils and bad
coffee—rocking chairs—three-way lamps—night running down
our face like mascara—a big bearded stranger with a book of
poems in his lap

WHY RALPH REFUSES TO DANCE

He would have to put out his smoke.
        At this time of year the snakes are slow and sorry-acting
His ice would melt. He'd lose his seat.
        you don't take chances once in a while you still see
He does not feel the beat.
        a coontail tied to an aerial, but don't look
His pocket could be picked. His trousers rip.
        for signs keep your black shoes on the floor
He could break a major bone.
        burn every tick you pull off your head
He remembers the last time he stepped out on the floor.
        roll a set of steel balls around in your fist
Who do you think I am, she said, a broom.
        looking at the moon's punched-out face
No, he mumbled, saxophone.
        think about Lily coming down the staircase
At the tables they whispered about him.
        her crushed-velvet chairs
He would begin to smell of baby shrimp.
        her pearled brown toes
The music could stop in the middle of his action.
        that time with the three of them in a boat
What would he do with his hands.
        and him throwing up in the river
The women his age are spoken for.
        as she stood up to skim his hat into the shallows
After sitting out so long, his heart could give out.
        and tomorrow would unleash another spell of spare-rib theology
People will be stepped on. A fight ensue.
        aw shuddup somebody clapped a hand on his shoulder
The cats in the band will lose respect.
        aw shuddup he was getting the heavy hand again
He will bring dishonor to his family name.
        are you going to dance or not, just say
good-night, no thanks, hallelujah yourself, go to hell.

OUR DUST

I am your ancestor. You know next to nothing
about me.
There is no reason for you to imagine
the rooms I occupied or my heavy hair.
Not the faint vinegar smell of me. Or
the rubbered damp
of Forrest and I coupling on the landing
en route to our detached day.

You didn't know my weariness, error, incapacity,
I was the poet
of shadow work and towns with quarter-inch
phone books, of failed
roadside zoos. The poet of yard eggs and
sharpening shops,
jobs at the weapons plant and the Maybelline
factory on the penitentiary road.

A poet of spiderwort and jacks-in-the-pulpit,
hollyhocks against the toolshed.
An unsmiling dark blond.
The one with the trowel in her handbag.
I dug up protected and private things.
That sort, I was.
My graves went undecorated and my churches
abandoned. This wasn't planned, but practice.

I was the poet of short-tailed cats and yellow
line paint.
Of satellite dishes and Peterbilt trucks. Red Man
Chewing Tobacco, Triple Hit
Creme Soda. Also of dirt daubers, nightcrawlers,
martin houses, honey, and whetstones
from the Novaculite Uplift.

I had registered dogs 4 sale; rocks, dung
and straw.
I was a poet of hummingbird hives along with
redheaded stepbrothers.

The poet of good walking shoes—a necessity
in vernacular parts—and push mowers.
The rumor that I was once seen sleeping
in a refrigerator box is false (he was a brother
who hated me).
Nor was I the one lunching at the Governor's
mansion.

I didn't work off a grid. Or prime the surface
if I could get off without it. I made
simple music
out of sticks and string. On side B of me,
experimental guitar, night repairs, and suppers
such as this.
You could count on me to make a bad situation
worse like putting liquid makeup over
a passion mark.

I never raised your rent. Or anyone else's by God.
Never said I loved you. The future gave me chills.
I used the medium to say: Arise arise and
come together.
Free your children. Come on everybody. Let's start
with Baltimore.

Believe me I am not being modest when I
admit my life doesn't bear repeating. I
agreed to be the poet of one life,
one death alone. I have seen myself
in the black car. I have seen the retreat
of the black car.

HUMIDITY

There are no houses no trees there is no body
    of water. Things are as they seem.
They are driving around another beltway of light.
A hand glows under the radio's green dial.
Both are taken up with their own itinerant thoughts
about the borrowed binoculars or mineral rights
to an unknown relative's land. They are at a point in space
where animate dark meets inanimate darkness.
Flares from refineries ignite their faces.
    There are no houses no trees…
Pods of satellite dishes focus on an unstable sky.
Soon they will exit and look for a café
where there are people. We'll hear them order
charcoal and beer, watching the fan work the smoke.
They could even take a room, and submit
unto the soaked bedding with one hundred strokes of night.
Here where imperfection gives way to perfection.
Things are as they seem. There are no houses
    no trees and no body of water.

The Body's Temperature at Rest

While you are walking across the Orient
in a yellow paisley shirt,
I go around the house
killing flies the rain drove indoors.

I sit in the shade drinking ice water.
When I bend to pick up paper against the fence
it blows into brown stalks of the cosmos;
I can feel you leaning back on your heels
chewing on the good times and the bad.

Mornings I dip a cold biscuit in the black coffee
and look out at the new shoots.
Before the tower blinks into view
I'm up on the step in my pajamas caressing the cat.
It's only Tuesday, we both have our heads in our paws.

When night gets here the wind
whips breath out of the bushes
and there is nothing more to do
but go inside and shut the door.

Sometimes I touch the mirror in the dark
and think of the cold noses of my brother's dogs
or seeing myself flicker against the shadowed walls
I'm reminded of the Villines boy
trying to kiss my eleven-year-old lips.
Not much stirs on our block at this hour
unless a coarse hand brushes over some coarse hair.

I've been sleeping with all the pillows
in the house and a lead pipe. Doors bang.
By the tired light I read
The Rise and Fall of the Third Reich.
The same car rumbles around the block.

Since her wires were cut, the old
Republican next door doesn't budge
from her brick fort but under escort

in a heavy car. The mulberry threatens
the fence. The dark-complected girl behind us,
she's gone completely wild this June.

I imagine you there
standing among 100,000 irises;
here, where the beds have died back
and you are always up before me
with your face and genitals washed
seated at your desk with a straight spine,
a clear head—writing another version
in which irises are spreading.

If you come looking for me
and I'm not knocking daubers out of the rafters
or watching reruns over a light supper,
come down to the pond; nab another bottle
of Mateus. When it's cool like this
I sit on a log under your poncho
burping back at the frogs.

PERSONALS

Some nights I sleep with my dress on. My teeth
are small and even. I don't get headaches.
Since 1971 or before, I have hunted a bench
where I could eat my pimento cheese in peace.
If this were Tennessee and across that river, Arkansas,
I'd meet you in West Memphis tonight. We could
have a big time. Danger, shoulder soft.
Do not lie or lean on me. I'm still trying to find a job
for which a simple machine isn't better suited.
I've seen people die of money. Look at Admiral Benbow. I wish
like certain fishes, we came equipped with light organs.
Which reminds me of a little-known fact:
if we were going the speed of light, this dome
would be shrinking while we were gaining weight.
Isn't the road crooked and steep.
In this humidity, I make repairs by night. I'm not one
among millions who saw Monroe's face
in the moon. I go blank looking at that face.
If I could afford it I'd live in hotels. I won awards
in spelling and the Australian crawl. Long long ago.
Grandmother married a man named Ivan. The men called him
Eve. Stranger, to tell the truth, in dog years I am up there.

PLANKS

While we are all together under burring bulbs we would do well
to remember the wild rose in the pelvis bone. Albumen.
The accoutrements and utensils of love. And labor.
A soft robe. A solid teapot. Our talking guitar.
Why not go to a green field. Barefooted, hair unbound. And fill
our belly with short sweet grass. Cover the shorn shoulders
with new wool. Rid the body of its white implacability.
Bite down and hold on. Remember string light.

Remember lives on the periphery: the Indian in handcuffs.
The twin sisters who man the mausoleum. Or just standing in line
we could shut our eyes. Stop counting. Imagine:
the color Naomi Trosper wanted to paint West Memphis;
now picture West Memphis, gentian violet.
While we are starching our coats for their steel constructions
we could be shining the particulars; emery boards,
grasshoppers…, remembering the birth of our boy. The giant hibiscus.

The first feces, meconium. Forever bearing in mind why
we have been assembled. Remember pain. The night Yolanda lost her baby.
Bite down and hold on. Be ourselves chastened,
doing away with engraved gifts, boxes of miscellany.
Ignore the butcherbirds. The aims of the ruthless. Bad endings.
Breakfasts of Coca-Cola and cigarette smoke. Sabotage. Stay
down and let go. Of vain love. The frayed light. All together now.
The night Esmerelda came to town and laid an egg. Forget pain.

Alone and awake in our cells like a bird left without a blanket,
we would do well to find the wild rose in the pelvis bone; turn
our back on the figure in the undergrowth, the felo-de-se,
his draining face. Albumen. Let us go back to the green field. And lie down.

Eliminate strategies. The key to the handcuffs. Singing nail file. *Acrididae.*
Bury Yolanda's placenta. The pain. Esmerelda's egg. The pain.
Naomi's violet city. Childbirth. Our talking guitar. We must bite down
and hold on. Never mind learning to draw. The giant hibiscus.

U T O P I A

Inside of me
there are no cathedrals
even in the vaulted halls
where you thought you would come upon
some providential soul
letting go a cage of doves
there are only vaulted halls.

Inside of me
there is a period of mud,
flies and midges come with the mud
followed by a time of intense sun;
with the sun comes a cool room
furnished by a rotating fan, a typing machine.
While there is sun I type then I walk
often for long stretches
in search of hidden springs, curative herbs
or not in search of a blessed thing.

Inside of me
a stranger rubs its knees
against the palings of my ribs
someone who may be born to fail,
a drifter hunched over a cinder block
pitching rock at mounds of garbage,
someone who may catch and tear
like a plastic bag in a fence.

But beyond this zone
of tire heaps and oil drums
a clearing entertains one tree;
where you thought you would come upon
blades of steel light or where
you thought the doves would collect themselves
there is only enough soil enough blood
and seed good enough for one tree.

Toward the Woods

The ones who were there stood
at the ends of the body.

Afterwards
I was pronounced dead.

I was sore with cold.
Nothing was marked up or down.

On the way out of a dense white woods
I composed matchbook odes.

I dropped crumbs of fresh paper,
passed a woman who seemed to know

something about where I had come from.
"I talked to Arkansas last night," she says.

"It's 80 degrees there," she adds. Friendly.
"They had thunderstorms all week."

I was feeling better. Looking
suddenly forward to the unpondered night.

Before the trees closed in on me
I watched two boys fighting by the river.

First I wanted the featherweight
then the freckled one.

And I glimpsed the bottom
of my husband's long-nailed toes

as he flopped
off the bank like a gator.

Ah, there he is now, Forrest,
in the ultrasilent light of a new kitchen

sitting across from our son
who has at last outgrown his cradle cap.

They have arranged themselves
at a strangely shaped table,

and appear to be sharing
a mold of frozen food.

They are draped in a sarong or toga,
their penises scored with age.

Once he comes to live on the outside of her, he will not sleep through the night or the next 400. He sleeps not, they sleep not. Ergo they steer gradually mad. The dog's head shifts another paw under the desk. Over a period of 400 nights.

You will see, she warns him. Life is full of television sets, invoices, organs of other animals thawing on counters.

In her first dream of him, she leaves him sleeping on Mamo's salt-bag quilt behind her alma mater. Leaves him to the Golden Goblins. Sleep, pretty one, sleep.

...the quilt that comforted her brother's youthful bed, the quilt he took to band camp.

Huh oh, he says, Huh oh. His word for many months. Merrily pouring a bottle of Pledge over the dog's dull coat. And with a round little belly that shakes like jelly.

Waiting out a shower in the Border Café; the bartender spoons a frozen strawberry into his palm-leaf basket while they lift their frosted mugs in a grateful click.

He sits up tall in his grandfather's lap, waving and waving to the Blue Bonnet truck. Bye, blue, bye.

In the next dream he stands on his toes, executes a flawless flip onto the braided rug. Resprings to crib.

The salt-bag quilt goes everywhere, the one the bitch Rosemary bore her litters on. The one they wrap around the mower, and bundle with black oak leaves.

How the bowl of Quick Quaker Oats fits his head.

He will have her milk at 1:42, 3:26, 4 a.m. Again at 6. Bent over the rail to settle his battling limbs down for an afternoon nap. Eyes shut, trying to picture what in the world she has on.

His nightlight—a snow-white pair of porcelain owls.

They remember him toothless, with one tooth, two tooths, five or seven scattered around in his head. They can see the day when he throws open his jaw to display several vicious rows.

Naked in a splash of sun, he pees into a paper plate the guest set down in the grass as she reached for potato chips.

Suppertime, the dog takes leave of the desk's cool cavity to patrol his highchair.

How patiently he pulls Kleenex from a box. Tissue by tissue. How quietly he stands at the door trailing the White Cloud; swabs his young hair with the toilet brush.

The dog inherits the salt-bag quilt. The one her Mamo made when she was seventeen—girlfriends stationed around a frame in black stockings sewing, talking about things their children would do;

He says: cereal, byebye, shoe, raisin, nobody. He hums.

She stands before the medicine chest, drawn. Swiftly he tumps discarded Tampax and hair from an old comb into her tub.

Wearily the man enters the house through the back. She isn't dressed. At the table there is weeping. Curses. Forking dried breasts of chicken.

while Little Sneed sat on the floor beneath the frame, pushing the needles back through.

One yawn followed by another yawn. Then little fists screwing little eyes. The wooden crib stuffed with bears and windup pillows wheeled in to receive him. Out in a twinkle. The powdered bottom airing the dark. The 400th night. When they give up their last honeyed morsel of love; the dog nestles in the batting of the salt-bag quilt commencing its long mope unto death.

DETAIL FROM *WHAT NO ONE COULD HAVE TOLD THEM*

Naked in a splash of sun, he pees into a paper plate
the guest set down on the lawn as she reached
naked in a splash of sun into a naked sun splash
He pees into a paper plate a plate the guest set down
into a plate of white paper the guest set down He pees
into a plate the guest set down on the lawn in back of the airy house
a paper plate the guest set down He pees on the lawn
He pees into a white paper plate a living fountain of pee
a golden jet of pure baby pee from His seven month old penis
His uncircumcised penis not even one year old a jet
of pure gold into an uncircumcised splash of sun
a beautiful gold arc of pee in a splash of uncircumcised sun
naked in a splash of sun He pees into a paper plate
a white paper plate the guest set down on the airy lawn
in back of the airy white house into a paper white plate
weighted down with baked beans and slabs of spiced ham
the guest set down on the lawn in back of the white house
on the lovely expanse of lawn the guest set down the paper plate
on the lawn as she leaned forward in the canvas sling
of her chair as she reached out of her green sleeve
into a white paper plate the guest set down on the lawn He pees
as she reached out of her green butterfly sleeve
out of the beautiful arc of her iridescent sleeve as she
set down on the expanding lovely lawn a paper plate
He pees naked in a splash of sun as she reached for potato chips.

OLD MAN WITH A DOG

climbing the hill
in a heavy coat
to Sunset Manor
to comb his wife's
white clumps of hair,
muttering,
72 years,
what you cannot
end up with
in 72 years.
Eating at the stove
in his heavy coat.
Watching TV
with the dog.
72 years
on the heel of this
Christbitten hill.
72 years
he wonders aloud,
What will I do?
How will I live?

LIVING

If this is Wednesday, write Lazartigues, return library books, pick up passport form, cancel the paper.

If this is Wednesday, mail B her flyers and K her shirts. Last thing I asked as I walked K to her car, "You sure you have everything?" "Oh yes," she smiled, as she squalled off. Whole wardrobe in front closet.

Go to Morrison's for paint samples, that's where housepainter has account (near Pier One), swing by Gano St. for another bunch of hydroponic lettuce. Stop at cleaners if there's parking.

Pap smear at 4. After last month with B's ear infections, can't bear sitting in damn doctor's office. Never a magazine or picture on the wall worth looking at. Pack a book.

Ever since B born, nothing comes clear. My mind like a mirror that's been in a fire. Does this happen to the others.

If this is Wednesday, meet Moss at the house at noon. Pick B up first, call sitter about Friday evening. If she prefers, can bring B to her (hope she keeps the apartment warmer this year).

Need coat hooks and picture hangers for office. Should take car in for air filter, oil change. F said one of back tires low. Don't forget car payment, late last two months in a row.

If this is Wednesday, there's a demo on the green at 11. Took B to his first down at Quonset Point in August. Blue skies. Boston collective provided good grub for all. Long column of denims and flannel shirts. Smell of patchouli made me so wistful, wanted to buy a woodstove, prop my feet up, share a J and a pot of Constant Comment with a friend. Maybe some zucchini bread.

Meet with honors students from 1 to 4. At the community college I tried to incite them to poetry. Convince them this line of work, beat the bejesus out of a gig as gizzard splitter at the

processing plant or cleaning up after a leak at the germ warfare
center. Be all you can be, wrap a rubber band around your
trigger finger until it drops off.

Swim at 10:00 before picking up B, before demo on the
green, and before meeting Moss, if it isn't too crowded. Only
three old women talking about their daughters-in-law last
Wednesday at 10:00.

Phone hardware to see if radon test arrived.

Keep an eye out for a new yellow blanket. Left B's on the
plane, though he seems over it already. Left most recent issue of
Z in the seat. That will make a few businessmen boil. I liked the
man who sat next to me, he was sweet to B. Hated flying, said
he never let all of his weight down.

Need to get books in the mail today. Make time pass in line at
the P.O. imagining man in front of me butt naked. Fellow in the
good-preacher-blue suit, probably has a cold, hard bottom.

Call N for green tomato recipe. Have to get used to the
Yankee growing season. If this is Wednesday, N goes in hospital
today. Find out how long after marrow transplant before can visit.

Mother said she read in paper that Pete was granted a divorce.
His third. My highschool boyfriend. Meanest thing I could have
done, I did to him, returning a long-saved-for engagement
ring in a Band-Aid box, while he was stationed in Da Nang.

Meant to tell F this morning about dream of eating
grasshoppers, fried but happy. Our love a difficult instrument
we are learning to play. Practice, practice.

No matter where I call home anymore, feel like a boat under
the trees. Living is strange.

This week only; bargain on laid paper at East Side
Copy Shop.

Woman picking her nose at the stoplight. Shouldn't look,
only privacy we have anymore in the car. Isn't that the woman

from the colloquium last fall, who told me she was a stand-up environmentalist. What a wonderful trade, I said, because the evidence of planetary wrongdoing is overwhelming. Because because because of the horrible things we do.

If this is Wednesday, meet F at Health Department at 10:45 for AIDS test.

If this is Wednesday, it's trash night.

WEEKEND IN THE COUNTRY

How water is run
or
a hoover

a new hinge is put on the trunk
or
a screen tears

Machado is read maybe

a jar breaks
or
a mirror

during an electrical storm
trees drop their fruit
or
some boards fall down

a walk with the 16 year old dog
or
a nap an apple a black and white tv

too much sun
or
shade

sitting in the yard after dark
a lightning bug in your hair
or
digging a hole for the dog

swim
or
avoid water and low wire

hanging the straw hat on a nail
or
throw it on the chair

cut your bangs
or
let your hair grow out

drive to town for liquor
and a movie
or stay in for macaroni again

humming under the umbrella
en route to the mailbox
or
sleeping late

morning over a cantaloupe
and a day old paper
or today's paper and no melon

another search
for the wristwatch
or
an address on a hardware bill

hearing things
or
a pot turns over on the porch

unexpected company
or
tipped back in a ladderback
watching ants
climb up your arm

More years pass and the book does not leave the drawer. According to our author the book does not begin but opens on a typewriter near a radiator. The typing machine has been aimed at the window overlooking a park. It's been oiled and blown out. At heart it is domestic as an old washer with the white sheets coming off the platen. In the missing teeth much has been suppressed. In the space and a half, regrettable things have been said. Nothing can be taken back. The author wanted this book to be friendly, to say, Come up on the porch with me, I've got peaches; I don't mind if you smoke. It would be written in the author's own voice. A dedication was planned to Tyrone and Tina whose names the author read in a sidewalk on Broad. The machine's vocation was to type, but its avocation was to tell everyone up before light, I love you, I always will; to tell the sisters waiting on their amniocenteses, Everything's going to be fine. And to make something happen for the hundreds of Floridians betting the quinella. It would have dinner ready for people on their feet twelve hours a day. And something else for the ones making bread hand over fist, the gouging s-o-bs. But the book was too dependent. Women were scattered across pages who loved the desert, but moved into town to meet a man. The women, understand, weren't getting any younger. Some of these women were pecking notes into the text when the author was out walking. One note said: John Lee you're still in my dreambooks, et cetera. The author had no foresight. In previous drafts the good died right off like notes on an acoustic guitar. Others died of money, that is, fell of odorless, invisible, utterly quiet wounds. The work recorded whatever it heard: dog gnawing its rump, the stove's clock, man next door taking out his cans, and things that went on farther down, below buildings and composts, all with the patience of a dumb beast chewing grass, with the inconsolable eyes of the herd. Basically the book was intended as a hair-raising document of the organisms. Thus and so the book opens: I have been meaning to write you for a long long time. I've been feeling so blue John Lee.

SELF PORTRAIT ON A ROCKY MOUNT

I am the goat. Caroline by name. Née 6 January. Domesticated since the sixth century before Jesus, a goat himself.

We have served as a source of meat, leather, milk, and hair. Our flesh is not widely loved. Yet our younger, under parts make fine gloves.

Out of our hair—pretty sweaters, wigs for magistrates. Our milk is good for cheese.

We share these gifts with Richard Milhous Nixon, who gained national prominence for his investigation of Mr. Hiss.

We're no sloth, full-time workers at the minimum wage. We had an annual income last year of $6,968, a little less than your average subway musician.

Our horoscope assures—we will be a great success socially and in some artistic calling.

We are surefooted, esp. on hills. We live on next-to-nothing. This week's victuals: ironing board covers and swollen paperbacks. Our small hills of filings fall under the heading of useful by-products. This we call Industrial Poetry. Both of us being Bearded, Mystic, Horned.

THE OZARK ODES

Lake Return

Maybe you have to be from there to hear it sing:
Give me your waterweeds, your nipples,
your shoehorn and your four-year letter jacket,
the molded leftovers from the singed pot.
Now let me see your underside, white as fishes.
I lower my gaze against your clitoral light.

Rent House

O the hours I lay on the bed
looking at the knotted pine
in the added-on room
where he kept his old Corona,
the poet with the big lips—
where we slept together.

Somebody's Mother

Flour rose from her shoulders
as she walked out of her kitchen.
The report of the screendoor,
the scrapdog unperturbed.
Afternoon sky pinking up.

Table Grace

Bless Lu Vindie, bless Truman,
bless the fields
of rocks, the brown recluse
behind the wallpaper,
chink in the plaster,
bless cowchips, bless brambles
and the copperhead, the honey locusts
shedding their frilly flower

on waxed cars, bless them
the loudmouths and goiters
and dogs with the mange,
bless each and every one
for doing their utmost.
Yea, for they have done
their naturally suspicious part.

Girlhood

Mother had one. She and Bernice racing for the river
to play with their paperdolls
because they did not want any big ears
to hear what their paperdolls were fixing to say.

Judge

Had a boyhood. Had his own rooster. Name of Andy.
Andy liked to ride in Judge's overall bib.
Made him bald. This really vexed Judge's old daddy.

Arkansas Towns

Acorn
Back Gate
Bald Knob
Ben Hur
Biggers
Blue Ball
Congo
Delight
Ebony
Eros
Fifty-Six
Figure Five
Flippin
Four Sisters
Goshen
Greasy Corner

Havana
Hector
Hogeye
Ink
Jenny Lind
Little Flock
Marked Tree
Mist
Monkey Run
Moscow
Nail
Okay
Ozone
Rag Town
Ratio
Seaton Dump
Self
Snowball
Snow Lake
Sweet Home
Three Brothers
Three Folks
Twist
Urbanette
Whisp
Yellville
Zent

Lake Return

Where the sharp rock on shore
give way to the hairy rock in the shallows,
we enlisted in the rise and fall of love.
His seed broadcast like short, sweet grass.
Nothing came up there.

Dry County Bar

Bourbon not fit to put on a sore. No women enter;
their men collect in every kind of weather
with no shirts on whatsoever.

Café at the Junction

The way she sees him
how the rain doesn't let up

4-ever blue and vigilant
as a clock in a corner

peeling the label from his bottle
hungry but not touching food

as she turns down the wet lane
where oaks vault the road

The Boyfriend

wakes in darkness of morning
and visits the water

lowering his glad body
onto a flat rock

the spiders rearrange
themselves underneath

Remedy

Sty sty leave my eye,
go to the next feller passing by.

Porch

I can still see Cuddihy's sisters
trimming the red tufts
under one another's arms.

Bait Shop

Total sales today: 3 doz. minnows, ½ doz. crawdaddies, 4 lead lures,
loaf of light bread, pack of Raleighs, 3 bags of barbecued pork skins.

Fred

One of your more irascible poets from the hill country.
Retired to his mother's staunch house
in Little Rock after her death; began to build
a desk for Arthur. Beautiful piece
of work. For a friend. Beautiful.
Drinking less, putting on a few pounds.

Lake Return

Why I come here: need for a bottom, something to refer to;
where all things visible and invisible commence to swarm.

for Fred

A FARM BOY (2005)

A FARM BOY

Who could have told
that the forebears of ernie edward wright would have rumbled
and rutted their way over the mountains of north carolina
and tennessee to plop themselves down in arkansas
in clay county around piggott then haul their modest belongings on up
to the snake-threaded hilly tangle of rock that is the ozarks
to clear enough land to raise a log house
that would by and by burn and then raise another
log and box lumber house this one with two rooms a long level porch
to bring up the five boys of james robert and lu vindie who foresaw
that robert and vindie who had six grades of schooling each
which in those days meant about eighteen months total
would leave the farm in 1926 to try their inexperienced hand
at cotton-picking in spiro oklahoma where vindie who was a williams
had some kin that had dribbled over the state line from the ozarks
only to discover they were better at growing and harvesting
big boy tomatoes and loading them onto a wagon to haul
to cisco's cannery to sell for eight dollars a ton
and that robert the father would hate the water in oklahoma
and hate the cotton and hate the brown land it was planted on
and come down with chills and sore joints
and determine to press on to joplin
birthplace of langston hughes
though that didnt mean beans to the wrights and the williams
for robert to work his way through another leg of his poverty
that so resembled the poverty of others
and get himself a job at a plumbing supply outfit and send for
his family to come to joplin by train where my father
ernie edward would attend his first town school
uncle harold would get born
and get to live in his first house with a flush toilet
that was the second house in joplin they rented
who saw that roberts appendix would burst
and he would almost die and have to come back to the farm in cisco
to convalesce and resume growing big boys and pole beans
and corn which calls for a lot of water and whatever else
you could get the dirt to yield
in those hills that the thorn trees and the neighbor boy
raymond fletchers lifetime collection of junk

would eventually overtake totally overtake
christforsaken acres and acres of human junk
so that ernie edward would come to stop at raymonds
trailer some sixty years later and raymond would
ask his boyhood friend with whom he used to set up a table
in the woods to play cards far out of vindies jurisdiction
until ernies brother troy would track them and
the rocks would start zinging by their ears
in the middle of a deal and ernie would sit down
to help his old pal raymond write out a will when
he ernie edward was up walking those hallowed hills
with his son and his daughter visiting his birthspot
and ernie and raymond would have to sit on the tailgate
of his truck because the junk inside his trailer rendered it
humanly un-enter-able and impassable and un-sit-down-able-in
and the same goes for the cab of the truck
they had to sit on the tailgate long enough for raymond
to scribble a holographic will
whereby the good smelly country fellow left his ample land
and his beloved junk to some distant dim relative
in real need and who would have imagined that ernie
and his older brothers harley and troy and
his younger brothers audie and harold bell
named for the aviator and popular writer of that totally
cornball book shepherd of the hills
would pass on through the one room school
in braswell springs and a bus line would start up just in time
to make it possible for ernie edward to attend
the greater metropolitan berryville high school
in which he excelled because he was a determined country kid
a determined child of the depression time
with a mind that clicked and sparked with an avidity
to put all the available learning
in his path to work to build a mind in the lost
hardwood reaches of the hills a singular hard-driving mind
who would tell that the depression would force
berryville high school to begin charging tuition at the start
of his junior year and ernie have to go before the principal to say
he would not be returning next year as he could not
his family could not they just did not have
the ten dollars for his tuition and the principal

knew this boy should go on and wanted him to go on
and thought ernie an adult name for a baby dont you think
and said now ernie dont you have anything you could sell
to cover the tuition and ernie said no sir just a little bull calf
and the principal said i'll buy that bull calf from you
for ten dollars and ernie knew it wasnt worth but three
four at most but he wanted to go and he wanted to go to school
in the worst way and so he did sell his little calf and he was
unmistakably the valedictorian of his class and that meant
he could go to college he would go to fayetteville
to the university and make a lawyer
as he already knew he wanted to make a lawyer
because he had visited the court often enough
before in berryville and even old claude fuller who
had a stranglehold on politics in carroll county was
worth watching because he made up for want of
a real legal grip with an uncanny sense of tactics
and that after all is part of the trial lawyers skill
working the room and claude wasnt short on
knowing how to work the room
roping the emotions wending through a dingy
courthouse full of overalls and spittoons
so then ernie went to college and had in mind to make
a lawyer and he and his brother audie who was
of the same mind and ernie and audie were going to be
partners by god and they were going to be
crackshot lawyers just like his dad robert was a crack shot
and could hit a squirrel in a tree with one shot
one eye shut and thats what they were going to do
by god and ernie he excelled in college because
he had a burning mind and it burned to learn
like langston hughes who grew up in the corrosive
racial chasm of his country
with his head in the comfort of books
and a teacher from berryville had a brother
who was a city attorney in fayetteville and
that good fellow set ernie up with a room in the firehouse
with seven other college boys from the country
to live in the firehouse and put out the fayetteville flames
and he also swept some stairs of an insurance office
on the square and he washed dishes on dickson street

where his only son and his only daughter would
also come for beer and company in their time
where his son for a short term was known as the batter spice man
at campbell soup and his smart alecky daughter would take
short orders at the d-luxe from the little drunk
in the porkpie hat known as the unofficial mayor of dickson street
and all three would hang out at georges majestic lounge
for beer and company in their own time
in fayetteville where ernie even ran a cast of white rats
through mazes at the sci lab
in honestness he despised those rats though he ran them
you know just about anything to earn
a quarter and he hung on in there
even though one professor told him he would starve out
and he left the firehouse to live
in a cooperative house run by the f-h-a
where the boys could donate canning and
whatever else was in their family larder
in kind for room and board and ernie was already
something of a figure on campus
he was already involved in political matters
like keeping the public phones free
and keeping the fraternities
from running everything and like taking the razorbacks
over to eureka springs in a borrowed truck
for a poll watch to break claude fullers stranglehold
until he graduated and got to go to law school
so he and audie could be partners
but audie just got through two years of law school
before he was enlisted in the airforce
until his plane was shot down over italy
the fine calf leather boot of italy
which took his fine blond body out of the sky
and ernies and audies attorney dream
went to complete smithereens
who wrote home when flying missions
over northern Africa
with all the curiosity of an inquisitive young man
witness to the living color of the world
for his very first time
and I quote from his letter of march 11 1943

By this time farming should be in a big way and religion getting lax while yelling gee and haw on the hillsides; so it is with the Arabs in this section. The principal crop in these parts seems to be wheat and other small grain and believe you me it is getting beautiful now with the rolling plains getting green with wheat and winter oats. The

Arabs use donkeys and I mean little ones. The jennies back home look like monstrosities compared with these. They too have camels that they use primarily for freighting purposes. It is most difficult for me to explain in details about their customs for as yet I have been unable to master their language; thus it is hard to learn very much by observation….

I have been in Algiers, Marrakech and other points which are censorable. If you locate these positions on the map, you will gather their strategic importance and will also be able to guess at their scenic grandeur both places are very beautiful…. There are lots of nice French people near here, but there too yours truly has three strikes against him for he took the wrong language in school….

Though a young man in years, I am an old man in experience…it will be a simple matter for me to settle for nothing in the hills of Arkansas—would that I could.

and that dream was blown
and ernie would never get over it and
robert would never get over it and
vindie would grieve until the end of her
nearly ninety years for her poor beautiful boy
whose life was built out of the same
tendon and gristle as ernies whose mind
was supple and perfect too
so ernie had no choice but to redouble his efforts
to make a lawyer a double good lawyer
to honor his dream and that of his brother
whereas like many a good mind before him
he had been loathe to kill even an enemy
the enemy now was just those that killed audie
while heretofore he had been a pacific person
oh he had fought a man at georges majestic lounge
who put a black snake in his bed just for fun
and that put him in a state to fight alright
but first he went home to change his shirt
because there was only the one good shirt
and he didnt want to ruin it
but he came back in his alternate shirt
and who knows anymore

who got the best of that one
putting a snake in your bed is definitely
a fight-stirring offense
but audies death that was the big one
so then ernie joined up and
they posted him to colorado
with his big flat country feet
his poor country eyesight
his poor enlarged country heart
in colorado there wasn't much action
to put your shoulder to just p-o-ws just ragged
thin whipped men just young diminished men
boys really who had fought
in their virulent leaders virulent war
but ernies mind could serve and it did and
his young wife alice served too and said
once in a while the young women
in the secretarial pool at the p-o-w camp
would leave candy or a stick of gum
out on the ledge of their desk for the prisoners
filing past to snitch as they were just
young beaten hangdog men boys really
being fed by their monstrous kampf into the maw
of history from which ernie and alice
would hope to spare their first born
their one son ever having to follow
for they now had a son of their own
named warren whose tendon and gristle
connected and his eyes blue-burning and true
in the awesome rockies and of course
when it was over and it was soon to be over
and while they were admiring of the rockies
they were expected to come back
to the purple-heart-filled hills of home
where ernie would soon hang his legal shingle
in the dam town of mountain home
which was soon to prosper
because they were building a dam
and his wife would learn
the profession of court reporter
and she and her friend fern would

become the twin crackshot
court reporters of the ozarks
and fern herself was a dam kid
and mother was a railroad kid
and ernie the farm kid
would begin leaning
into the tawny bindings of his law books
and really never weary of
the letter or the spirit
because he knew and was educated in his marrow
to uphold the framework
of what is often misnomered as civilization
by being a citizen
by being an unintentional hero
which is almost always misnomered
by being a discerning practioner
of the greater precepts
of justice and equality
because he was educated in his marrow
to know it takes practice practice a lifetime
of practice

JUST WHISTLE

a valentine (1993)

THE BODY, ALIVE, NOT DEAD BUT DORMANT, like a cave that has stopped growing, stirred up, awakened, waked, woke itself altogether up, arose to a closed set of words, *I wish you wouldn't wear your panties to bed,* the body, on its flat feet, breaking into sweat, breaking into rivers, unbent at five and one-half feet, having slept, as if in a boat, where the hair on its legs continued to curl long and gold, where its papers were stored, more or less dry, in a can, where whatever grew tired or useless fell off, fell away, having been not dead, but dormant, living, slept as if in a boat, oarless, unmoored, sand pouring out of a canvas bag,

SAND SEEPING FROM CAVITIES NO LONGER MOIST, not
removing the panties, but making every effort to conform to
the hull among scales, and leaves from overhanging willows,
weepers, older than them even, wept, wounded into dormancy,
unable to plug the wound, water deeper than night, the lewd,
newly enlivened wound, night deeper than water, wound older
than the body's marrow, older than its rocks, dogs glomming
along the unstable rocks of its words, stirred up by days,
sunblare, dreaded as the vulture dreads its own shadow; then, a
slightly taller body waving from the shoreline with an armadillo
on its shoulder, waving wildly as if for the pantied body to pull
to rocky shore and share the armadillo, as if they had not
crowed the night before

THE PANTIED ONE SAID NOTHING, not even its own newly
enlivened name, its own naked name, the memory fulgurant,
sheet lightning of other bodies, of the one that did not have a
book in its house, the one that kept running to the pot, the one
that admitted it loved the boat, the body stayed because it loved
the boat, the impartial body, the inseminator, the second
inseminator, the one over which the body had cut itself, just
whistle cuts, the one that did not end after the aspirin incident
but only much later during the war, our war on them, not the
grunt the dodger, the one that ended in a hospital among
neotenous bodies caparisoned in black, the first inseminator,
the quick wit, that thespian, that did not attend the
termination, the dropout, the redneck, the uncut one, the juicy
one a subway musician, the second inseminator, that did not
attend the termination, the liar, the other liar, liar of liars,
pants on fire, the gentle one, the only gentle one, the rough
kisser, the one with an indefatigable hand, the all-night rover,
that readily laughing one, their combined tongues and clavicles,
the two drunks, the original liar, so that even after the liar died,
slew itself, eleven years after the liar died and had not a
second's thought about its own rotted body

MUCH LESS THE BODY IN PANTIES, the thinnest issue of piss
seeping through, staining the sad panties a touch more, despite
the cavernous question, so what was the big g-d deal anyway,
why not repudiate the worst and resume, there must be a cure,
some sweet acidophilus, poppy juice, a pill…, but that had to
have been before the solecistic remark about the panties, which
the body had not really noticed so used was the body to the
cloth, the plight of their facticity, the elastic in the legs and the
waist not being felt, the discoloration having blended them
perfectly with the flesh, no line or hair, neotenous, and there
being very little moisture, except for the thinnest issue of piss,
it considered itself piquant; now this unmistakable run in the
heretofore seamless nights, a disturbance as with a stick in the
water, a seiche, this mention, this soft utterance in the dark
where the one body could not be sure the other body was
present but for the insistence of vowel points,

IT WAS A DEFINITE RUPTURE in the zone in which they
interpenetrated with decreasing frequency almost without
knowing it or as the one had been told of a flier so virtuous the
flier could maintain zero gravity in our air, rolling a big jet
without passengers knowing they had been rolled,
apocryphal or not, if a body coming through the haulm were
willing to help the body scaled and riddled with mistakes, to
help the crumbling, hacky, runny body, the stiff, fitful body, the
dumb, anachronistic body, the teratogenic, totally gnarled,
hobbled body get to the other shore,

In the Old Days

we didn't have this and we didn't have that
We rolled down the sloping shadows
Into the blue hollows like a bottle
Swallowing grass and stems
We fell into a nest of harmful bodies
We were pale and far as the sun
The harmful ones went sleeveless
Like trees without leaves
How we loved their smooth torsos
Like bluffs we leaped off
We loved them rough as boards
Hard as rocks we loved them
We had a voice soft and filmy as a mussel
We were like farm kittens
Each one different but the same
Our love was like the pulp
Of luscious fruit
We put up with a lot
Like living on Tchoupitoulas
That was the old days
Who could have penetrated the fog
In such bodies in those days

A Brief and Blameless Outline of the Ontogeny of Crow

Tonight one said   Bluets the other said

Goosefoot one said   Hungry the other said

Hangnail it said   Spanish bayonet it said

Daylilies it said   Hotel it said

Matches it said   Sickle senna it said

Feverfew the one said   Headache the other said

Panties it said   Panic grass it said

Clotbur it said   Backdoor it would say

Tickets the one said   Purslane it would say

Morning glories said one   Money said the other

Whistle it said   Asshole it thought it said

THE ONE WATCHING THE OTHER ONE a long time before it
got up, the one shoving a pillow under the plums of the other,
the one not removing the panties even *in situ;* once this identical
thing happened out west where so many beat families set down
their beat gear and did their levelheaded best to get rid of one
another, trampling the succulent ice plants; then *ex nihilo* the
one who was asked not to wear the panties to bed was told to
go check on the dogs

IN THE BODY'S OWN WORDS, it cannot live like a vegetable in the country, it no longer cares if it does die do, let them take a crowbar to its valves, let them open the howl of its os on the rocks, *why don't you go put your hands in some water,* the body is urged, but it chooses to celebrate its firing with a smoke

ITS CARELESS POSTURE, its long trunk, its howling os, for so
long it has been accused of bruxism, of failure to perform on
the pot, of fulgurating, of hoariness, of bags; there are things
which happen to it only at night, but the body dare not repeat
them, the better to disguise its beastliness, while its ferns
continue to brush their fronds off the porch, the cat cries and
cries to be let out, then cries and cries to be let in, the body has
been prepped, no need to shave everything, what doesn't take
too long is over too fast, the body is possessed of childlike
fears, predominantly flat fears, the armadillo does not respond
to its calls, a phone rings and rings, the book opens, the letters
take off black as flies, it fulgurates, love *avec* disgust, time
divided by mercy, who is its shepherd, crow minus love, has it
any wool, what on earth could be keeping it

BECAUSE CONDITIONS ARE IDEAL FOR CROWING the singers
flock to this spot. They rageth they seizeth they penetrateth
and maketh us to lie down by the roaring waters. By day they
take the longstem roses to our backdoor. They secure us to
trellises. They whip us breathless. This includes the pool
painter whose hands are perpetually blue. Aquatic. Transbluent.
One hand signs the blued canvas of our body. Other hands.
Cigaretted. Hired hands. Dripping paint on the plush carpet.
They set a different set of teeth to each teat. Spit like
grasshoppers. In the eden of their woods, dogs glom. Warm
winds stir them up. They let the flightless birds peck our feet.
We hold mirrors. Bloody our lip under the rent in the
backdoor. They crow us for the quick and the dead and on
the third day they rise and crow us again. Very soon now we can
return to our life of wonder and regret.

DESK CUTS

I am incredibly sad

You bought a guitar
To punish your mother
You bought a kazoo
To punish your cat

        whacka
        whacka

I am a slave of the society

If love is blind
And God is love
And Ray Charles is blind
Is Ray Charles The One

        whacka
        whacka

BFS kicks major butt

O love like a meteor
Falls from such a height
At such a rate
Leaving such a hole

Now I am really stuck

        whacka
        whacka

Inseminate them

Book Titled *The Ballad of Sexual Dependency* Found in the Hydrangea in front of Zorabedian's Stone

A photograph ripped out

If a fist of pennies is buried
alongside the bowl, the hydrangea
will grow blue

Zorabedian must be an Armenian name

Odds are a thousand-odd to one
the absent photo   was a crow shot

O the ballad of sexual dependency
is very old and intensely sad
we learned it before we learned

To bury a fist of pennies
alongside our bowl
could turn one's   abundant bushes blue

That Zorabedian was an Armenian is also true

DUSTY APPLES IN A DUSTY KITCHEN. Ferns brushing their fronds. Sound of water. Sloshing. Body atop an ice-cream parlor chair. Finger tracing salt on the table. The body on its hinges. Midafternoon hysterics. What does the body want. For God's sake? What a lousy situation. A good whipping. A night or two in the pokey wouldn't hurt. To meet another body coming through the haulm. Swinging its plums freely. Awhistling.

THE BODY TAKES OFF ITS JEANS IN THE BARN. Washes its
face in webs and rain. The hair on its legs curled gold. Checks
to see, are its papers dry. More or less. Panties riding high.
Checks the sprung trap. Stroking the little belly. Soft and still.
The other body asleep in its fields. The armadillo on its sleeve.
The indelible smell of the harmful ones. Not the one who
worked for the highway department painting the center line.
Yellow glo-paint coating its hands. The bold yellow signature
on the gessoed canvas of the body. The musty undies below the
waist. Ladder to the loft. Barn light. Bestirred. Benastied. Crow.

THE ONE WENT SO FAR AS TO SEND AWAY for another body
in the mail. The response was overwhelming. The one poured
over the contents in the bathroom. Sound of water sloshing.
Settling for the time being on an ascetic dish from France. The
prevailing respondent wasn't French but frenched and smoke-
free. The settlement was supernumerary as in the famous rib of
lore. The initiator was inclined toward limerance, a delicious,
venial condition (which is achieved without reflection or
consent and so according to Thomist theology does not deprive
the soul of sanctifying grace) nonetheless causing widespread
perturbation in the system of the body left akitchen gnawing on
its hinges.

GLARINGLY INSIGNIFICANT. Predominantly flat fears. Go put your hands in some water. Light a fart. They all rise up and leave their hairs on the pillowcase. They all enter breath's cul-de-sac in their own precious time. The body does not mourn its former bodies. The body leaves its ossuary for others to tend. Yet the body leans back on the trunk of an old friend, and says, Because it is beautiful here, because it is so grotesque, because it is useless, vitiate it, slay it here. Now.

FOLLOWED BY ANOTHER CLOSED SET OF WORDS, *I just want
you to last,* when already the unlasting has started, ruts have
formed, petechiae, bags, dents, lacunae, sloughing, discharge,
rot, the blaze between the cheek and the jaw, gouged-out areas,
new growths, horrible excrescency, discoloration, elongated
lobes, the buildup of wax, crud, the degenerate mortar of lime,
hair, and dung, whilst the beckoning of the thousand-odd boats
in the bay, the glisten and alternate glow of a fresh brainpan in
a fresh apron, the identical age, not one cold flick nor hot lick
older, its neotenous allure, doll-like, not a museum, no old
familiar crow, predominantly young and manifest, with its
thousand-odd reifications of its own solid grey matter, wielding
authority, improvements in every direction, advances, actual sea
lions at sunset, their seductive facticity, meanwhile the body on
its pantied hinges in its kitchen, biting into its dusty apple,
gnawing around the worms, wondering if it couldn't be useful
yet going door-to-door

ADVANCE OF THE DISTINCT BODIES behind the partition, the
death of day, the rupture of motors, contamination of news,
lightblare, sloshing sound, the time-honored tool ever alert
under its suit, the long-maligned tube manufacturing trouble
under its folds, the frisson of their proximity, the ineluctable
concussion

The body is a suspect
in the offense of crow. It has the right
to remain naked. It does
not have to give a statement or answer any questions.
If it gives up its right
to remain naked, anything it touches
can and will be touched against it
on a floor of needles and moss. It is the forest's
hoary wife. It has the right

to the presence of a crow
and to talk with the crow
before and during its coring.
If it cannot afford a crow
and it wants one, one will be anointed for it
at no cost to it before coring.
If it does talk to the big guns it can stop
at any time.

The big guns made no threats
or promises to it. The body understands
its rights. It is a suspect.

According to the author of *Points
for a Compass Rose* all of us are
defined by three transcendental
experiences: sexuality, aesthetics,
and violence. Given the world
is not mean it is brutal,
Rosa's death comes to mind.
Who cut her teeth on cane. In the haulm.
Her breasts hacked off.
She voided into her apron. They closed in.
Crowed. Slew her in the haulm. She was flensed.
We, the transcendentally defined, climbed
back into our rental cars.
Given we do not heal but harden,
our eyelids pushed down as if by a big darkness.

NO. IT WORST. DESTROYS. None. Possibility. Pitched. Of. Friendship. Past. With. Pitch. Others. Of. It. Grief. Insures. Its. More. Isolation. Pangs. It. Will. Neglect. Its. Schooled. Body. At. Abandoned. Forepangs. No. Wilder. Longer. Wring. Is. Comforter. Anything. Where. Few. Where. Crimes. Is. Entail. Your. Worse. Comforting. Punishment. Cries. Than. Heave. Generous. Herds-long. Fault. Huddle. Of. Woe. Putting. World-sorrow. Oneself. On. Entirely. Age-old. In. Anvil. Another's. Wince. Hands. And. Where. Sing. Where. Sing. Is its shepherd. And. What. Is. What is. THE THING. Keeping. IT.

WHILST THE ONE BODY referred to its wound as IT another designated it THE THING. Both bodies did long battles with their wound and the body referring to its wound as IT slew itself on the eve of its own birthday whilst the one designating its agony THE THING gave birth to itself, took its children in hand and visited the sea. Very likely IT and THE THING are one and the same. Very like the felo-de-se had access to something the parthenogeneticist did not. Had the felo-de-se held out a little longer, the fog would have dutifully burned off, and it too could have visited the sea. In the old days, picnics, socials, public whippings, hangings, and spelling bees were amusements in which the entire family could partake. But no one, in those days, able of body and soul, stood up in its saddle and let loose with a panegyric to its hole. At point-blank range. At least not in mixed company.

HOLE OF HOLES: world in the world of the os, an ode, unspoken, hole in its infancy, uncuretted, sealed, not yet yielded, nulliparous mouth, girdle against growth, inland orifice, capital O, pore, aperture to the aleph, within which all, the overstocked pond, entrance to vast funnel of silence, howling os, an idea of beautiful form, original opening, whistling well, first vortex, an idea of form, a beautiful idea, a just idea of form, unplugged, reamed, scored, plundered, insubduable opening, lightsource, it opens. This changes everything.

AND NOTHING. The body slept under the bow two nights.
Propped up with an oar. Cocked its gnarly head and listened to
sheet metal music. Birds swooped down on it. The rock on its
chest getting bigger. The wind told secondhand lies, more lies.
It felt a breeze enter its vestibule. The flesh had begun to grow
over the elastic in its panties like bark over fencing. Several of
its fingers fell off, fell away. Oh well. It would not end up like
the others. In a typing pool. Splitting gizzards. If necessary a
prosthesis could be fashioned out of lime, hair, and dung. It
could still crow.

On the Eve of Their Mutually Assured Destruction:

The body would open its legs like a book
letting the soft pencils of light
fall on its pages, like doors
into a hothouse, belladonna blooming there:
it would open like a wine list, a mussel, wings

To be mounted without tearing:
it would part its legs in the forest
and let the fronds impress themselves in the resin
of its limbs, smoothen the rump
of the other body like a horse's. To wit:

The whole world would not be lost.

Let the record show the body
has made identical claims before
though never in the wake of its flensing.

CONTRACTIONS THROUGH THE NIGHT. Further and further apart. Then not. Contractions through the following night. Contractions. Closer and closer. Then constant. Two fingers. Scored. A long hall of bodies propped before televisions. The rupture of motors. Contamination of news. Lightblare. A bed. In which to bring forth. Impossible to lie flat. Walk. Walk the long halls. Counting televisions. Impossible to walk. The nub of the bone rubbed. Incessant rubbing of the nub. Up-to-the-minute machinery. Advance of the machines. Relief of rubbing. Respite of ice. Through the night. Rock on its chest imbedded. Getting bigger. Tremendous fall of rock.

At the Lying-In

Spell your last name for me please
                        P-a-r-k-e-r
What do you do
                        I am a shipper
How far did you go in school
                        10th grade
What does your husband do
                        He killed himself
Did you intend this pregnancy
                        You know what people do in pairs
Do you have any other children
                        4 boys
Were any of those pregnancies planned
                        We were just kids
                        I don't regret it
Have you been drinking during this pregnancy
                        Only rum & coke
Do you smoke
                        I am trying to cut back
Approximately how much do you smoke
                        Less than two packs
What did your husband do
                        He moved rocks

THE CORPSE WAS IN THE BED. On its back. The eyes were
slipping back into the head. The lids were shutting down.
Entrance to vast funnel of silence. It was dressed in a white
shirt and white shorts. There was very little blood. A few
bottles of beer. Chicken wings on the end table.

On the Morn Of

The body would shut its eyes like blinds
letting the nearly even lines of light
steal away from its sheets,
straight gold hair astreaming there;
it would close like a glass door, an ear, arms

To be folded without crossing:
it would seal its lips on the forest
and let the teeth impress themselves in the skin
of its fruit, feast upon the marl
of the other body like a wilderness. To wit:

Its whistling world would be not harmed.

Let the record show the body
has never made such plaintive claims before
except in the wake, the wake of.

Here that sad body lies with its rubymeated vestibule
    receiving the breeze.

The other body, priapic as a cigar, rubs the dark-staining juice
    on the areolae.

Lights conk off as they pass.

One thing, the panties have to go...

It knows its rights it has been a suspect many times before.

Darkness parts the multiple folds about the hole. The windows
    come down in unison.

Nevertheless, it is very perturbing all this business
    with the cigar and the areolae.

In the first place, the panties have to go ere it is too late.

First, promise this isn't going to be any mustache job.

Ere it is too late...

If a body really wanted to help a body get to the other shore,
first it would have to take the panties, go back get the body
bring the panties back and get the cigar...

Staple it to the armadillo,

THEN DIG. Curl itself up at the approach of wheels,
    uncurling as they spin off in unison.

The leaves are dry enough for a nest;
    the ground gives.

The body will be walking in hours
    though the shell will be yet soft.

It might ring the armadillo
    and thank it. Thanks (for pointing out

This unmistakable run in the heretofore
    seamless nights, a disturbance

As with a stick in the water, a seiche,
    this mention, the accidental

    eden of its words).

PAIN WITHOUT WALLS: progressive pain: effacement of walls:
four fingers: cored: a lot of hair: the pull the pain: the reaming:
exhaustion: the rupture: contracting: ceaseless pulling: pressure
of rock on chest: hair seen through the vestibule: tremendous
fall of rock: absence of space: of breath: lights conk out as they
pass: plummeting like a meteor: in unison: vast funnel of
silence: dark parting the multiple folds about the hole: spinning
into darkest surround: final vortex: plummeting into absence:
from such a height: idea of beautiful form: intense monitoring
of form: lights conk out as they pass: beautiful: darkness:
spinning:

the needle: the needle is in: fear of needles: old childhood fear:
old predominantly flat fear: it is a very old very fearful child: it
is in distress: air absent: fear: fulgurating: fear *avec* pain:
radiating distress: *avec* pressure: wheeling through a corridor of
light: wheeled at tremendous speed: the windows come down in
unison: needle entering the spine: wheeling into steel light: it
freezes: freezing in the steel light: it freezes: teeth clicking: slit:
emptied: released: glossy god brought to the head: golden:
gorgeous: great gust of love: shown to the head: gone: gushing
blood: an actual flood: absence of breath: of form: a beautiful
idea: expelled: blood sloshing down the steel stilts: blood
spilling onto the tile: seeking the drain: at such a rate, more blood:
blankets: hot blankets and blood: teeth clicking in the head:
limbs rattling on the steel: stainless-steel music:

the fat apathetic clock on the wall: what country does this
mean: *why don't you check on the dogs:* what language does the
clock talk: see if you can count the bodies in this surround:
blankets: a stack of hot blankets: thanks: thanks so much: is
there a lot of blood: and blankets: is love king: is it The One:
help count: the clock has something to do with the country: the
country of blind kings: there are any number of bodies in the
bright surround: then less: slit: emptied: expelled: released:
move out now: let's move: every body let's go: every: body: gone:
leaving such a hole

A PARTITION SEPARATES IT FROM OTHER BODIES: a calm is
coming: the promise of calm is calming: the body a yellow and
blue canvas: swollen: distended: yellow and blue mixed gives
green: the other body wipes the leavings from the swollen
distended body: not a word on the armadillo: the gorgeous god
is set upon an aureola: loveblinded: they are: in the country: it
is: golden: of the blind: they are: kings

OVER EVERYTHING: up through the wreckage of the body, in its troughs, and along its swells, tangled among its broken veins, climbing on its swollen limbs: a blanket of fresh, vivid, lush, optimistic green; the verdancy rising even from the foundations of its ruins. Weeds already amid the bruises, and wildflowers bloomed among its bones. Everywhere were bluets and Spanish bayonets, goosefoot, morning glories and daylilies, purslane and clotbur and panic grass and feverfew. Especially in a circle at the center, sickle senna grew in extraordinary regeneration, not only standing among the blown remnants of the same plant but pushing up in new places, among distended folds and through rents in the flesh. It actually seemed as if a load of sickle senna had been dropped. On the eighth day…

Is it. is it.
it is. it is.
an object of worship.
graven.
an object of contempt.
craven.
asshole it thought it said.
whistle it said. just whistle.

VOICE OF THE RIDGE

Something about a hazy afternoon—a long drive
    about cedars spearing the sky
Something about a body at a crossing
    about a dog missing a paw
    about buying a freshly dressed hen
Something about the locus of the dead

Something about a strange town on a weekend
    about large white panties on a line
About a table in a family-owned café
    an old morsel on the tines
Something about the owner dragging one foot
Something about wine from a jelly glass

Something about a hazy afternoon—a long drive
    about no purse no stockings
Something about unfolding the map
    about a cemetery that isn't kept up
    about grasshoppers—their knack for surprise
Something about finding a full set of clothes in the weeds

Something about a hazy afternoon—a long drive
    about hills of goldenrod
Something about filling-station attendants
    the one blue hole in the clouds
Something about birds of prey—the locus of the dead

Something about the long drive home—a slow sundowning
    about the din of insects
Something about straight gold hair on a pillow
Something about writing by the kingly light
    in the quick minutes left before lips
    suction a nipple from wrinkled linen

AS IF A FIST OF PENNIES had been buried alongside its bowl, *at least it didn't have to be funny for this one,* its bush bloomed blue, the one rooting, eyes shut, not Zorabedian, one was just out awhistling through the Armenian burial ground, the abundant bush, bent to pluck the book of photographs, this ballad is known by all, crow shot ripped out of the middle, it is very old and intensely sad, the panties excoriating in their own precious time, a healing beat begun, sheet metal music, revealing the sunlit shaft, the glans, crura, the other body's extreme *soif,* the thinnest issue of piss, arid as the hydrangea, the other body planting its pennies, a soul kiss, febrile, acoustic, an armadillo waddling off on its own, the other body inclined toward shade, fulgurating, alongside the bowl, asking could it have some of that water, the other roused, if only temporarily, waked from its amniotic dreaming, unbent at five and one-half feet, flicked the switch on its vestibule, *did you check the dog...* suspicious, fulgurant, but passing through its fluorescent words to the perineum, perpetrator of crow, fueled by previous experiences, where crow nearly slew it, deadening pedagogy of crow, not feed on thee, no, for if the body meet a body coming through the haulm, the boat aground, for all of them so loved the boat, site of their facticity, occasion of the angel's wee victory over the beast

It was so lifelike it was uncanny

it had its own ontogeny

the sequestration of the suspect nearly over

it arrived like a blot-from-the-blue

it stayed on, a macula on the forehead

etiolating their days of wonder and regret

the big guns arrived but it was too late

it had no alibi

thoughts of its dying cheered us up

a soft utterance in the dark

a night or two in the pokey

years in a leaky boat

were nothing compared to the beat of this wing

The pitch of the body   unbent

    risen on an elbow   its abundant bushes

its hills of goldenrod and especially in a circle at the center

    sickle senna   in brilliant darkness   a fresh apron

in extraordinary regeneration   touched against

a nerve of tender concern   for its papers

    its incredible fingers   flattening them

one at a time   a healing beat   begun at point-blank range

    around the insubduable opening   the leaky wound

seven inches down and especially along the edges of its realm

    the frisson of their proximity, the ineluctable concussion

They Sleep

with tenderness, wracked

heaving

outspread

They Sleep

heaving, outspread

with tenderness

wracked

THEY SLEEP

outspread, heaving

wracked

with tenderness

TREMBLE (1996)

FLOATING TREES

a bed is left open to a mirror
a mirror gazes long and hard at a bed

light fingers the house with its own acoustics

one of them writes this down
one has paper

bed of swollen creeks and theories and coils
bed of eyes and leaky pens

much of the night the air touches arms
arms extend themselves to air

their torsos turning toward a roll
of sound: thunder

night of coon scat and vandalized headstones
night of deep kisses and catamenia

his face by this light: saurian
hers: ash like the tissue of a hornets' nest

one scans the aisle of firs
the faint blue line of them
one looks out: sans serif

"Didn't I hear you tell them you were born
on a train"

what begins with a sough and ends with a groan
groan in which the tongue's true color is revealed

the comb's sough and the denim's undeniable rub
the chair's stripped back and muddied rung

color of stone soup and garden gloves
color of meal and treacle and sphagnum

hangers clinging to their coat
a soft-white bulb to its string

the footprints inside us
iterate the footprints outside

the scratched words return to their sleeves

the dresses of monday through friday
swallow the long hips of weekends

a face is studied like a key
for the mystery of what it once opened

"I didn't mean to wake you
angel brains"

ink of eyes and veins and phonemes
the ink completes the feeling

a mirror silently facing a door
door with no lock no lock

the room he brings into you
the room befalls you

like the fir trees he trues her
she nears him like the firs

if one vanishes one stays
if one stays the other will or will not vanish

otherwise my beautiful green fly
otherwise not a leaf stirs

Approximately Forever

She was changing on the inside
it was true what had been written

The new syntax of love
both sucked and burned

The secret clung around them
She took in the smell

Walking down a road to nowhere
every sound was relevant

The sun fell behind them now
he seemed strangely moved

She would take her clothes off
for the camera

she said in plain english
but she wasn't holding that snake

SO FAR OFF AND YET HERE

Because I know this is going to be painful
I can feel the pain before it acquires a shape

      Now nearer to me

How at night it is just audible
like mice in the insulation

So windows snow and pears soften
an old house settles into its infested studs

Always there is more inside
than outside in the open

Where I came to be identified with
your scars and green limbs

      Now nearer to me

What in the meantime happened to my eyes
they shone   at least   they seemed capable   of shine

But a poem on a page by itself
does not penetrate the retina of fear

      Now nearer to me

So the mind dispels us
radiators gasp and washers wear out

Your left middle finger sinks inside me
the nail of love just holds

LIKE PEACHES

change   speak   sway
keep lingering smell
protected by a succulent seal   a bur
yield one's earthly wand   one's earthly sac   into this vessel
trace   blaze   clear
the foliage at the wrought gate
the serrated tongue   rescinded   along with the dream
of urinating in three streams
sunscalded

Forever Lynne   riddles the water tower   of a dying town
ripen   cling   drop
what would it be like to fell   this mess of twigs   to graft
the shaking body   to lyric   the seasoned body   to stem
to shake   the lyric body   to season
the stemmed   to trail   the fallen…
slather   shudder   lower
drupe

things that are not written in this book
don't go boring your nose in the fork of a tree not even present
arise   refreshed   wormed
pulpy   opaque   ecstatic
lingering innocence
of perfect nexus   shave the epicarp   collect the juices
we orchard

WITH GRASS AS THEIR WITNESS

Not more lonely than the road
    the women who loved him
Not more beautiful than the road
    the men who loved him
He came in behind the rain
    seated himself under your trees
Clutching his genitals in one hand
    he emptied his green mind
      How beautiful were those men
whose tongues went over the ridge
    of his balls how lonely
the water left standing in the road

BECAUSE FULFILLMENT AWAITS

An arm reaching back through a hole in a ceiling
for a box of poison   "Now"   the dark talks
"I hate being a man"   An arm offering a box of poison
in the direction   of a hole in the ceiling
A handkerchief offered   "Wait"
comes the warning from below   "Cover yourself"

Even in touching   retouching
steeped in words   in the proliferation and cancellation
of words   one tends to forget   one forgets
the face   the human face   One wants
to create a bright   new past   one creates it

AUTOGRAPHS

This is blood: close with your lover and bite down
Bear in mind: this is a duet
I'll drive: shift your excellent body under mine
Ideal environment: lush, well-lubricated
Neighborhood of origin: sells cigarettes, schnapps, lotto tickets
Weather: late ozark spring
Soft entry: it can be done
Strangest device: cock rings
Preferred intervention: human hand
Source of common terror: retina
Wish: to never know unhappiness again
State flower: bearded iris

Site of their desire: against a long high wall under vapor light
Most likely to succeed: the perpetual starting over
Inside his mouth: night after night after night
Directive: by any means necessary
Song: "Anarchy in the U.K."
Sign: hibiscus falls off the ledge
Nightmare: actual horse seated on your ribs
Sonic relations: silent, breathy, ululant

Recurrent fantasy: trickling between his legs
Cutest ass: bend, cleave
Religion: against my fire
Kismet: I feel very fortunate
Abstraction: leaves out too much
Biggest flirt: some people have roman noses,
      some have roman hands
Secondary concern: depilation

Eau de toilette: white shoulders
Rambone: I need it I need it now
Back of her throat: slit light
Second wish: compassion
Depth: valley's proper
Other sites: corridor, phone booth, shower, elevator,
      locker, filling station, boat dock, drive-in, cafeteria line
Most unlikely position: autumn dog
Regrets: all the dumb things I've done

Saving grace: clear out of own accord
Goal: revanchism
Plans for the future: to be a great success socially and
      in some artistic calling
Third wish: that his fingers remain agile
Future: went kind of nuts when still a relatively young man
Last date: when he stopped touching her, jan 4
Best dancer: hands down
Mantra: no one has been hurt, no one has been killed

P.S.:   have a wonderful summer and a wonderful life

And It Came to Pass

This june 3
would be different

Time to draw lines

I've grown into the family pores
and the bronchitis

Even up east
I get by saying goddamnit

Who was that masked man
I left for dead
in the shadow of mt. shadow

Who crumbles there

Not touching anything
but satin and dandelions

Not laid his eyes
on the likes of you

Because the unconnected life
is not worth living

Thorntrees overtake the spot

Hands appear to push back pain

Because no poet's death

Can be the sole author
of another poet's life

What will my new instrument be

Just this water glass
this untunable spoon

Something else is out there
goddamnit

And I want to hear it

GIRL FRIEND

When I first saw her a few summers ago I felt.
               Her photogenic spit.
I was climbing a coruscating staircase.
In my flammable skin. To be so full of.
Everything. At her age. It is very difficult.
A singer manqué. Among a small host of poets.
               Noisier
than the men. Quaffing schnapps. No lens
could describe her.
               Shoulders. Hands.
Such longings: Errant. Verdant.
To have a good time. And dream. In one's own
country. The lack. Of. Everything.
The confusion. It is very difficult. One needs.
One's own set of golden books. What if.
A ladder were. Miraculous. Extended. Across
a nursery for new stars.
               And then.

for Nina

SONIC RELATIONS

In the space of an ear
she told him the uncut version
in all but inaudible detail
without motors without phones
he gathered round her
like books like chairs
her warmth her terrible warmth
flooded the tone

That summer she began again
my sunflowers stood as tall
as girls on ladders
she mentioned ralph and fire
twice mentioned ralph
and the fire
across an azimuth of space
her warmth her terrible warmth
flooded the tone

She paused he was sweating
as though he had transported her
on his shoulders the whole summer
all over the county
she looked at him like some hair
she kept wrapped in cloth
doors slammed a book fell
he gathered round her

Her warmth her terrible warmth
flooded the tone
without motors without phones
he saw ralph then and the fire
in all but inaudible detail
he looked at her
like some combs he kept
wrapped in cloth

"We love it here" she said
"The girls are glad
the sunflowers and ladders
even the broom the eggs are glad
the air is so sweet
the water is sweet"
she looked at him
across an azimuth of space
he gathered round her
her warmth her terrible warmth

Various Positions

It was getting on toward suppertime

It was his night off

A shoe dropped

It had nothing whatsoever to do with you

It was an efficiency apartment

The breast seeks its own level

The table got down on its knees

With an amaryllis at their sill

They assume late spring donkey

It was stifling

It is the hair that makes it so mysterious

A book of matches goes off in her shirt

He wants nothing more than to sleep

Inside her holster

The chair fell to pieces

On the eve of the eighth day

Her milk came in

THE SHEPHERD OF RESUMED DESIRE

one steps forward   under a sifter of light
holding a globe   in ungloved hands   we share
the experience   of dying   in snow   pages turn
on illuminated fragments   we become   aware
of the extremes: joy   and   revenge   the fierce
confusion therein   one form senses another
when there is pressure   from all sides   and wasn't the light
seminal   tilting toward us   nay,   labial
we knew from the start   the center was within us   this blizzard
this conversation   could go on   for years: should you

go   should you stay   no shoulds about it   no matter why
the hole was made   the task is not yours   to fill it
why standest thou   so near   to the brink   how old were you
when you first lay down   before the god of love   what was
the objective: a staff   against the wolf   of reality
nay,   to get warm   only to get warm   would you be
let down again   if I said   it were not the one true god
but only a candle   of the same   where were we in the mid-
dle of a phrase: we froze we fell we went to a gilded hell
I only have escaped to tell you   though I have come to be lost
I do not ask you to lose your own self   in my triangle   only
to keep watch   yea,   to keep watch   over the shaping
of the sky   snow orbiting   all   abide abide

Oneness

As surely as it is about air
    about light and about earth

Water will seep between fingers
    gathered in a gentle fist

For what good a wooden fence
    against breath fuming with fire

What good to point out the flower path
    if the sugar bag is empty

What good blowing the clarinet
    if blowing only makes one ugly

For as surely as wind unlocks
    car doors and cabinets

Young men wander off with their testes
    to part the perineum's grasses

And when they come to the little stream
    each tenses against the other

And against anything unforeseen
    and under each pair of skin

She discovers his unassailable otherness
    and under each pair of skin

He discovers her moisture, dark, fecundity
    for as surely as it is about air

About light and about earth
    gathered in a gentle fist

Water will seep between fingers
    for the unknown must remain unknown

GIFT OF THE BOOK

lights go off
all over
rhode island
everyone falls
into bed
I stay awake
reading
rereading
the long-awaited
prose
of your
body
stunned
by the hunger

GIRL FRIEND POEM #2

Awake ye and come to our house
Come running   fly if you can

The doors throw themselves open
The name for this part is hearth

Today is the best day since yesterday
We share   a sense of rivers

Amazed at what we saw
We thought we were dreaming

The eyes the eyes
The golden domes they've beheld

The annihilating smile
The year you married the falcon

Here an hour follows an hour
One glass of wine deserves more

So it is not paradise
Everybody enters the green

At nightfall   modestly clad
Calling their children

Everybody has somebody
For whom to cry

for Frances

A SERIES OF ACTIONS

Like someone who has given

The gift of blood

The skin of the face is shining

Arms fold around each other

A string leads the way

Cold is the floor that receives
    the feet

The movements by which one
    accedes to the door

The handle inscribed in the hand

The door opening on the scene
    of shoelaces   eyelashes

The left hand keeps it focused

The door opening on the living
    almost unbearable

Light inside the space

The door opening as the palm
    of an eye

SONG OF THE GOURD

In gardening I continued to sit on my side of the car: to
drive whenever possible at the usual level of distraction:
in gardening I shat nails glass contaminated dirt and
threw up on the new shoots: in gardening I learned to
praise things I had dreaded: I pushed the hair out of my
face: I felt less responsible for one man's death one
woman's long-term isolation: my bones softened: in
gardening I lost nickels and ring settings I uncovered
buttons and marbles: I laid half the worm aside and
sought the rest: I sought myself in the bucket and won-
dered why I came into being in the first place: in gar-
dening I turned away from the television and went
around smelling of offal the inedible parts of the
chicken: in gardening I said excelsior: in gardening I re-
quired no company I had to forgive my own failure to
perceive how things were: I went out barelegged at
dusk and dug and dug and dug: I hit rock my ovaries
softened: in gardening I was protean as in no other
realm before or since: I longed to torch my old belong-
ings and belch a little flame of satisfaction: in gardening
I longed to stroll farther into soundlessness: I could al-
most forget what happened many swift years ago in
arkansas: I felt like a god from down under: chthonian:
in gardening I thought this is it body and soul I am
home at last: excelsior: praise the grass: in gardening I
fled the fold that supported the war: only in gardening
could I stop shrieking: stop: stop the slaughter: only in
gardening could I press my ear to the ground to hear
my soul let out an unyielding noise: my lines softened: I
turned the water onto the joy-filled boychild: only in
gardening did I feel fit to partake to go on trembling in
the last light: I confess the abject urge to weed your
beds while the bittersweet overwhelmed my daylilies: I
summoned the courage to grin: I climbed the hill with
my bucket and slept like a dipper in the cool of your
body: besotted with growth; shot through by green

LAKE ECHO, DEAR

Is the woman in the pool of light
really reading or just staring
at what is written

Is the man walking in the soft rain
naked or is it the rain
that makes his shirt transparent

The boy in the iron cot
is he asleep or still
fingering the springs underneath

Did you honestly believe
three lives could be complete

The bottle of green liquid
on the sill is it real

The bottle on the peeling sill
is it filled with green

Or is the liquid an illusion
of fullness

How summer's children turn
into fish and rain softens men

How the elements of summer
nights bid us to get down with each other
on the unplaned floor

And this feels painfully beautiful
whether or not
it will change the world one drop

On the Beach

"I cannot help you"   was the message
inside the green bottle   her footprints
dissolving in dry sand   to the spaces
between words   she assigned various meanings
the father flew   toward the daughter
his terrestrial body borne lightly by its cushion
clutching a poke of tomatoes on his knee
alone   with the beating of his own heart
      he didn't really mind living

      in the unseasonal heat
of her kitchen she held the pitcher of tea
against her cheek   wanting a breeze
the miniature wheel by the bed   ceased
to spin   "Courage and sex"   he said
setting his poke down   at last   "Caroline,
is all love is"   finally   with a faint sound
as a loneliness sewn by hand   the wing
sheared away   finally the loneliness   sheared
      away   as a wing sewn by hand

WHAT KEEPS

We live on a hillside
close to water
We eat in darkness
We sleep in the coldest
part of the house
We love in silence
We keep our poetry
locked in a glass cabinet
Some nights We stay up
passing it back and
forth
between us
drinking deep

Key Episodes from an Earthly Life

As surely as there are crumbs on the lips
of the blind   I came for a reason

I remember when the fields were no taller
than a pencil   do you remember that

I told him   I've got socks older than her
but he would not listen

You will starve out girl   they told her
but she did not listen

As surely as there is rice in the cuffs
of the priest   sex is a factor   not a fact

Everything I do is leaning   toward
what we came for   is that perfectly clear

I like your shoes your uncut hair
I like your use of space too

I wanted to knock her lights out
the air cut in and did us some good

One thing about my television set it has
a knob on it enabling me to switch channels

Now it is your turn   to shake or
provoke   or heal me   I won't say it again

Do you like your beets well-cooked and chilled
even if they make your gums itch

Those dark arkansas roads   that is the sound
I am after   the choiring of crickets

Around this time of year   especially evening
I love everything   I sold enough eggs

To buy a new dress   I watched him drink the juice
of our beets   And render the light liquid

I came to talk you into physical splendor
I do not wish to speak to your machine

GIRL FRIEND POEM #3

She was white and flown
as a kleenex turning into a swan.
I lifted her veil; the face disappeared.
As if I had exposed some film
to sun. Twirling our skirts.
Laughing until the clouds sopped up
the light. And the peaches fell down around us.

for Sharon

IN A PIERCING AND SUCKING SPECIES

he doesn't see anybody
in the tree
nor does she see anybody

in the grass he wires
that wiring her
he gets erect

reading this very wire
in the grass
she gets wet

the presence of his absence
disturbs the absence
of his presence sometimes

more sometimes less
in dreams they go forward
without hunger without faces

others fall off the limb
but she does not fall
she pierces him

everywhere and nobody else
when she returns
she seizes him

in quivering mandibles
relieved
to find him

unchewed
newly in leaf

CRESCENT

In recent months I have become intent on seizing happiness: to this end I applied various shades of blue: only the evening is outside us now propagating honeysuckle: I am trying to invent a new way of moving under my dress: the room squares off against this: watch the water glitter with excitement: when we cut below the silver skin of the surface the center retains its fluidity: do I still remind you of a locust clinging to a branch: I give you an idea of the damages: you would let edges be edges: believe me: when their eyes poured over your long body of poetry I also was there: when they laid their hands on your glass shade I also was there: when they put their whole trust in your grace I had to step outside to get away from my cravenness: we have done these things to each other without benefit of a mirror: unlike the honeysuckle goodness does not overtake us: yet the thigh keeps quiet under nylon: later beneath the blueness of trees the future falls out of place: something always happens: draw nearer my dear: never fear: the world spins nightly toward its brightness and we are on it

has been written in mud and butter
and barbecue sauce. The walls and
the floors used to be gorgeous.
The socks off-white and a near match.
The quince with fire blight
but we get two pints of jelly
in the end. Long walks strengthen
the back. You with a fever blister
and myself with a sty. Eyes
have we and we are forever prey
to each other's teeth. The torrents
go over us. Thunder has not harmed
anyone we know. The river coursing
through us is dirty and deep. The left
hand protects the rhythm. Watch
your head. No fires should be
unattended. Especially when wind. Each
receives a free swiss army knife.
The first few tongues are clearly
preparatory. The impression
made by yours I carry to my grave. It is
just so sad so creepy so beautiful.
Bless it. We have so little time
to learn, so much... The river
courses dirty and deep. Cover the lettuce.
Call it a night. O soul. Flow on. Instead.

GIRL FRIEND POEM #4

Together they will marry the man
who will not wear gloves

In the morning they throw hair
from their brush out the window

Now the birds have enough for a nest

A lot is moving
in the frangible life of the soil

Amid the susurrus of grasses
one chair waits near another

The public is in ecstasy

for Kate

THE IRIS ADMITS THE LIGHT THE IRIS WILL ALLOW

a letter flew into his hand
just like a bird into glass
undatable expressions
began crossing her face
he went up the ladder
to a heaven of solitude
an uneven seam of sunshine
stitched up her eyes

LIKE SOMEONE DRIVING TO TEXAS
BY HERSELF

a car   that could not pass inspection   an expired license
like someone suddenly overtaken   with a need to see them
   again   moving fast and in formation   she could feel
               the white lines
streaming by   the radio tuned to the road   like someone
   crying in the bathroom   she attacked her own idiom
            welcomed
   the distraction of corporeal detail   a toenail on the tile
some hair   the drain could not swallow   according to
   the legend   not a long way to go   books thrashing
in the trunk   unpowered steering   the arduous turning
           around
   and skies   amassing at the border

           words appeared
   by which she wanted to live   not singularly but
           companionate
in a wandering and guilty life   everyone makes
        orthographic errors
   while her face slept in her hand   her mind saw him
     sitting at his oak plane   with his new pen
he wrote steadily into the night   thinking the next paragraph
    would surely snuff out   the destroying angel
thinking the sequel to the rain would be a gaining movement
    focused between two cones of light
      like someone driving to texas

MORNING STAR

This isn't the end. It simply
cannot be the end. It is a road.
You go ahead coatless, light-
soaked, more rutilant than
the road. The soles of your shoes
sparkle. You walk softly
as you move further inside
your subject. It is a living
season. The trees are anxious
to be included. The car with fins
beams through countless
oncoming points of rage and need.
The sloughed-off cells
under our bed form little hills
of dead matter. If the most sidereal
drink is pain, the most soothing
clock is music. A poetry
of shine could come of this.
It will be predominantly
green. You will be allowed
to color in as much as you want
for green is good
for the teeth and the eyes.

LIKE ROCKS

they surfaced   gradually   until the center cooled
male and female colored differently   like dinosaurs
colored by impurities   autochthonous
sprung from inner earth   or ancient seas
without names   sunscreen   honorary degrees
given the climate
and the silence   except for continuous wave action
intermittent screeches
a strange yelping   impervious to   oarlock
axstroke   gunstock   out of pressure   heat from above
and under

continuous wave action   impressed with ferns
quarry me   uplift   butterfly me   micturate
across the flat of my back
it had to be a dawn horse
crag   fracture   cleave
fingered   sniffed   specified
by luster   hardness   coarseness
the caught and faceted light
rubbed smooth   by continuous wave action
in the very beginning   was only fucking
hunger   poetry   breath   shhhhhh

PRIVACY

The animals are leaving
the safety of the trees

Light sensors respond
to the footfall of every guest

To retard the growth of algae

The fishes must be moved
from the window

Stiller than water she lies
As in a glass dress

As if all life might come to its end
within the radius of her bed

Beyond the reef of trees a beach cannot be seen
the bay itself barely breathing

In the other wing of the house
a small boat awaits elucidation

GIRL FRIEND POEM #5

The brunette is boarding a train
with many bundles

The pockets are sewn shut on
her rayon jacket

The old world tapers away

The day slips through the straw
whole as an egg

We use Gregg shorthand
so the men won't understand

The brunette has traveled over 700 versts

A breath parts her lips

Let's nurse one another's babies
she says even before

We tell what we've been reading

for Shelby

PONDS, IN LOVE

One was always going when the other was coming back
One was biting a green apple
The deeper the evening the louder the singing
Throwing the core out the window
An oar stirred the dark and then quit
A face drenches itself in carlight
A wrist wearing a man's watch dipped a net
Even as one turned toward an unfinished building
The other wondered what one would have on
Upon returning will the hair be fallen or cropped
If one reaches what is grasped for
Gnats go for the eyes
Will utter disappointment set in
Will it be water or milk or wine tonight
Mostly one listened in the low-intensity glow
Of events one sustains incomprehensible feelings

LIKE HORSES

in their long black coat   they love the back roads
show their teeth   in a heartbeat   breathe in breathe out
don't fool around with them   their involuntary nervousness
beasts   of draft and burden   they are naturally
nervous   saps for the sweet sop   left buttock rubbed
against bark   and barbed wire
she ungulates   whence their fire   sweat like ballerinas
and stink   during the intervals
cannot help but be anxious   for the morrow   don't trust
anybody
they are helpless lying down

the young husband stands
on one foot   in front of the blackboard   the wet banged
equestrian students   breathe in breathe out   the sugar apple
on his desk   cannot help but be anxious
for the morrow
he ungulates   don't trust anybody   never have
they never will

FLAME

the breath	the trees	the bridge
the road	the rain	the sheen
the breath	the line	the skin
the vineyard	the fences	the leg
the water	the breath	the shift
the hair	the wheels	the shoulder
the breath	the lane	the streak
the lining	the hour	the reasons
the name	the distance	the breath
the scent	the dogs	the blear
the lungs	the breath	the glove
the signal	the turn	the need
the steps	the lights	the door
the mouth	the tongue	the eyes
the burn	the burned	the burning

GIRL FRIEND POEM #6

When I snap my fingers
You will wake in a dear yet unfamiliar place
You will scarcely remember your travail
You will be eating green caterpillars over a small fire
An awesome congeries of youthful men and women
Will be brushing these very tracks away

for Debbie

GIRL FRIENDS #7-10

THE REVOLVING HOUSE,
OR ANOTHER GIRL FRIEND POEM (#7)

The sitting women are sitting there
they are admiring what is there to admire

That whistling whistle in the breath
of the child as it escapes the child's oneiric head

Slowly they began to shift ever so slowly in motion

And swear they will tell no one of the things they see

So wandersome has been their ride so gladly they arrive

The vision they would limn of arches, visions
of ladders and other lofty animate things

The waving women are waving, they wave at you and me

They watch themselves in the water and the water
watches back waving at every other passerby

Spring Street Girl Friend (#8)

In the snug harbors, helicopter and electric eel
blink like stringlight in the pathetic, exhaust-resistant trees.
There has to be one more night like this, and then
peace and prosperity will reign for an even minute.
The vendor's hands don't look very clean, but we knew
it was a dirty city. The chestnuts smell deceptively good; we're
hungry even though they are mealy, and then
she comes down in her otis elevator holding a cricket cage.
She purposely wears the purple terrycloth robe of nobility.
The music scarcely changes up until now, and then
with the tiniest monogrammed scissors we snip
a ribbon of undergraduate hair.
She offers the food of her breasts.
She does not give a fig about our depression
glass; she's not into collectibles.
She does not rust or crack; up to this point
we know no more than two of the names under which she wrote
nor her intellectual milieu. The buddha
in the takeout emanates an unknown strain of mercy,
and then we get suddenly scared and tell the driver
we want transfers to the real world
where the fish smell like fish and the cheese like cheese.

CERVICAL JAZZ: A GIRL FRIEND POEM (#9)

In his worsted socks she followed

the clocks on their dissenting rounds
    of their Watertown apartment

There is not a cat nor is the fire lit.

The way the vitrine absorbs the blue light.

Softly, into a cordless phone:
    "Have you ever tried tiger balm."

The left ear follows the churn
    of a not-so-distant engine.

Nor a mirror on a wall.

A glass of wine at six, aerogram
    from the sister in Hungary:

furious holograph on life in the glove factory.

The blind street,

bowl of paperwhites…

Holiness only in living;
    this the tablecloth knows;

the pillowcase makes it so.

for Lida

Girl Friend Poem #10

She woke up in a hotel in the Green Mountains
    but was unaware of that yet

She woke up with a powerful, possibly drunken
    memory

She woke up sounding the walls of her memory
    for particulars

    letters from an incidental protagonist
    or a wooded scent

From the jagged shade of her pillowcase
    she turned

    from her own honey spot she turned

Even as it was being written she herself could see

a nameless woman holding a violin case
    tied by a woven belt

    the bridge damaged by thaw but in service

    the woman in the mist of the falls

an unidentified woman suspended
    in the brash blast of cascading light

DEEPSTEP COME SHINING (1998)

LEAR: …You see how this world goes.
GLOUCESTER: I see it feelingly.

Lead me, guide me to the light of your paper. Keep me in your
arc of acuity. And when the ream is spent. Write a poem on
my back. I'll never wash it off.

Meanwhile the cars continued in a persistent flow down Closeburn Road.

The refrain to the rain would be a movement up and down the clefs of light.

Chlorophyll world. July. Great goblets of magnolialight.

Her head cooling against the car glass. The mind apprehends the white piano, her mother. Who played only what she chose, who chose only to play, "Smoke Gets in Your Eyes."

A stadium emptied. The ruby progression of taillights. The eyes' ability to perceive a series of still images as continuous motion. Time lapse.

This wasn't movie traffic. There weren't twenty people to see *Smoke*.

At the drive-in. When they were young. The parents were young. The children falling asleep on the hood with the motor warm. Coating the ornamental swan with their prints. The projectionist's private life: shadows animating a wall.

"Never avert your eyes." (Kurosawa).

A photograph is a writing of the light. *Photo Graphein.*

More than magnolia, crepe myrtle is missed. The white bushes especially.

Against undifferentiated dark. It is unlike night.

She will still be up when we come in. Our floating host. She will be at the door in her pleated nightgown. Admit us into her air-conditioned nightgown. Her glory cloud.

In the seclusionary cool of the car the mind furnishes a high-ceilinged room with a white piano. Seldom struck. Color sensations. In which the piano floats on a black marble lake, mute swan in a dark room. Beyond the windshield the land claims saturate levels of green. Illuminating figures and objects. Astonishing our earthliness. I was there. I know.

Everyone in their car needs love. Car love. Meat love. Money love. Pass with care.

Deepstep, baby. Deepstep.

The boneman said he would take the blinded to the river. With a mirror. And then what.

The boneman said he would take the blinded into a darkened room. And put a hot-herb poultice on their sightless face.

Mullein for this mullein for that. We called it flannel.

Then leave them there.

The baby sister of the color photographer had a baby girl in the hills. Born with scooped-out sockets in the head. Born near the tracks they sprayed with Agent Orange. The railroad's denials, ditto the army's.

They would have been blue. The eyes. She did not have. Blue as the chicory in yonder ditch.

We see a little farther now and a little further still

She said her lights would be on and they were

Groping around the sleeping house in our gowns

Peeping into the unseen

Beautiful things fill every vacancy

Ripcord Lounge is up on the right. 32° beer. A little past the package store. Suddenly I have the feeling of a great victory. A delirious brilliance.

All around in here it used to be so pretty.

The boneman's bobcat. Its untamable eyes in the night. Did you
know a ghost has hair. A ghost has hair. That's right.

Peaches and fireworks and red ants.
Now do you know where you are.

I boarded with a suitcase of Blackbeard fireworks. I had
forgotten about the Unabomber. They shook me down.
Confiscated my sparklers, my roman candles, my ladyfingers.

Make a left just beyond Pulltight Road.

The land obtained in exchange for two blind horses. This land
became known as Wrens.

Merely listening

After the rain the trees smell so pleased

The hale sleep naked atop the sheets

We leave the deck for the lawn

The grasses licking our feet

A semicircle of chairs opens a parenthesis

In the direction of the lightsource

We see a little farther now and a little further still

Peeping into the unseen

Why is she so kind. Our floating host. Why am I so stingy
and vain.

A baseball diamond in every hamlet.

The waitresses in hairnets. Nurse-caps. Employees must pluck
out an eye before returning to work.

Cold eyes are bad to eat.

You lied. She doesn't have air conditioning. She is long in bed.
Note on the fridge: Vanilla yogurt inside. See you in the
morning, girls. How did you like *Smoke*. No one should know
the hour or the day.

We will become godlike.

Open the window. That the glory cloud may come and go.

Inside the iris of time, the iridescent dreaming kicks in. Turn off
that stupid damn machine.

Kepler's invention of the *camera lucida* fell into oblivion some
two hundred years. There is no avoiding oblivion.

Where does this damn stupid thing go. For god's sake. Are you
sure you want to wear that.

Especially in this one-stoplight town. Watch out for "the swerve
of smalltown eyes." (Agee) Feel them trained on you in unison.

Boiled peanuts. Now that is an acquired taste.

Once the eye is enucleated. Would you replace it with wood,
ivory, bone, shell, or a precious stone. Who invented the glass
eye. Guess. The Venetians. Of course.

Go to Venice; bring me back a mason jar of glass eyes. They
shall multiply like shadflies.

The antinomian marsupial in the road fixing us in her

eyeshine, *tapeta lucida*. The objective is hopeless—abandon

the baseball diamond for the strip mall. Nothing arboreal

to correct the view. The Dumpster behind Long John Silver's

berths the opossum in its postnuptial fast-food armor. Slower

now, go slow. SPEED   HECKED BY RADAR. O lucky stars.

Motel 6 left its light on for us. Remember you are nothing

without credit.

.

In Rome, (likewise-built-on-seven-hills), Georgia, the citizens hail their fellows as Romans. We never found the Forum. The arrows continued pointing right. And a sculpture of Remus and Romulus. Given by Il Duce to the Romans of Georgia. Stored in a root cellar during the war.

It follows that in Athens, Georgia, the citizens hail their fellows as Athenians.

West of Rome is Poetry. Poetry, Georgia. Wonder who lives there.

In the antique store, voices emanating from the pots.

How I miss the white piano. Only in the fovea. Where the photoreceptors are so concentrated. Maximal sight.

Keep me in your arc of acuity. *Siempre, por favor.*

Maybe you should turn the air conditioner off. We're not moving. The rain gives but brief relief.

I'd take the boneman over the snakeman, but when the snakeman talked about walking his six-pointed stag home through the pecan orchard, I felt a twinge of envy for the gentle living that can go on in the country. And when I peer inside the cage the boneman keeps the bobcat in, I feel a twinge of ill will toward his ignorance.

Deepstep. People just know what they know. (Come shining).

The chicken's name is Becky. They found her a good home with a peahen for fellowship. Chicken love.

Don't park in the shade on my account.

If we let the windows down we can hear Cape Fear. Exhaust stink. Or is that Hog Waste Lagoon. Man alive, that's foul.

Get your bearings. Hear the trees.

The silver threads of Spanish moss dripping from the telephone wires. It flies here. In pianolight. Like ghost hair.

Healers in these parts can make one WHOLE or deathly sick. If the swamp doctor pencils a series of random numbers on some bones you could win cash or a convertible. If your given name is penciled on a string of ribs. Whatever the swamp doctor says. Comply. Whether a believer or not. Remember Pascal shewed our very air has weight. It can be measured.

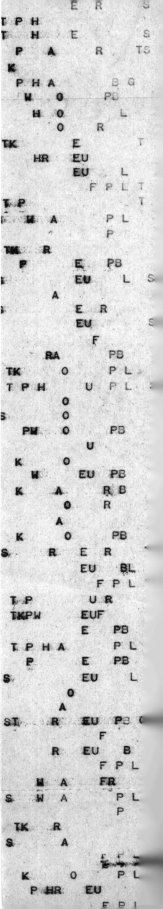

Writ by hand. Crudely executed. In the hopeless objective of receiving the marvels that come to one by sight, sound, and touch, merely in order:

To feather
To cream
To fall to the knees
To chicory
To fold
To coax (a tomato)
To keep a pet (antelope)
To rain but brief relief
To river
To shield
To watch
To fiddle (rain or shine)
To ride. To eat.
To have black hair.
To see to feel WHOLES
To stick out
To poke around
To spit
To bleach
To suddenly
To know the Veals (of Deepstep)
To sleep (hale)
To continue (in a persistent flow

It's the year of the magicicadae. Seventeen-years underground. Boring slowly upward. Ever so slowly. To get to the surface in the spring of the seventeenth year, it will scrabble through pavement. With not a minute to spare except for sex and song.

It must escape its carapace. Quickly. We must all escape our carapace. Come shining.

The day animals need to be able to distinguish colors. And the night creatures must manage low levels of light.

The white piano is her mother. And it fills with petals. Ghost hair. Who shot the piano. Killed the mother. And made the daughter to suffer.

The cat has guanine in the retina. Extra sensitive. In Yeats's version Oscar Wilde's father enucleates his patient's eye at the dining-room table and the cat eats it. "Cats love eyes," the cat lover reassures his patient.

Onion light. Vidalia onions. That's right. Now do you know where you are.

The boneman said apply flax and whites of egg to bleeding eyes.

So Gloucester had to smell his way to Dover.

But we aren't going there. Or anywhere the air does not smell of barbecue.

The preacher considers Whitey's Drive-In his parish.

What did you buy at the 20-cent table.

Where do you folks live at. Between the *a* and the *t*.

Take a mirror to the river. Then what. The young woman shuffles into the boneman's shed, and he brings her a jar of fermented swamp mulch from the closet. To make the swelling go down. Leglight.

First visual memory: one of vagrant white splotches in a clearing, a fat, diapered baby in a field of timothy chasing another diapered bottom through the timothy. Last visual memory: one of vagrant white splotches in a clearing, a fat, diapered baby in a field of timothy chasing another diapered bottom through the timothy. When it's mowed, and the fodder's fresh. I remember. I was there. No other features vex the view: Not the barn, the Gold Bond Medicated Powder sign fading from its highway plane. The black dog tearing after us. (*Night,* the black lab, the family's ecstatic.) The specific lighting from the sky never impinged upon the eye. Not individualized rocks. Split-rail fencing edged with fleabane. The proximity of a neglected pitchfork. Never never never…

Alligator couple bowed up and trolling the swamp alongside.
Can they reach the shore before we can reach the car door.
Watching them watching us plan our getaway.

This is where Michael Jordan's father napped in his Lexus.
Near Lumberton where Shelby's darling was born. Lexus love.

Everyone in their convertible needs love.

So what did you think of the movie *Smoke*.

I liked the business about Bakhtin rotting in prison, fresh out of
rolling papers. Smoking his manuscript.

Morning glories. What's your favorite.

Pull in at Chuck's Dollar Store I want to buy some Visine; some
X-acto blades.

The land obtained in exchange for two blind horses. This land
became known as Wrens.

If you bought that bobcat you could set it free. Then you would
need to go back and turn the dogs loose. They're just as
miserable. Pet one pet the other. And the chickens on top of
each other in the miniature coop in the Red Flyer. One of
those chickens could be Becky's kin. Chicken love.

Since he left my Red Flyer out for trash pickup I've been
shouldering one rock at a time. Never throw out any thing
whatsover on wheels.

He was here; then he was gone. He came for his money. Name
of Broomhead. I said, O go on.

Love it Leave it Love it Leave it Love it Love it Leave it Love it

And we all shine on.

The boneman hung up a sheet, slashed it, and ordered the
blinded one stick his arm through, then he stuck thorns in their
sightless arm.

There are enough signs. Of the lack of tenderness in the world. And yet. And yet. All you have to do is ask. Anyone here can extol the virtues of an onion. Where to get barbecue minced, pulled, or chopped. The hour of the day they have known the thorn of love.

I'm a little bit queasy about the boneman's acupuncture.

There may be an ordinance against clotheslines. In Shelby's old neighborhood, there was an ordinance against walking on certain streets with a lunch bucket. And on and on and on.

The sky, convict grey.

I didn't like the snakeman. He had a shitty attitude.

And if thy right eye offend thee pluck it out.

Love it Leave it Love it Leave it Love it Leave it Love it Leave it

Let him lay there, I wanted his headstone to read. What could I have been thinking. Even if his very words.

Where he is, in the utter absence of chlorophyll. How could he choose to be without trees.

We bought a string of bones from Bone Man that he cast a root curse on the developers; that they have a treeless afterlife. One endlessly paved forever.

If you have to go to traffic court, you can rent the boneman's staff which he brought from his father's native Haiti. It makes an impression in the courtroom.

Even the Copilia, a mere speck, perceives images.

Her fallen porches. Her non epitaph. Her other house invisible to strangers. Her manuscripts in the hands of warring kin.

When in Rome. Do as they done in Milledgeville. Once a bird sanctuary. That's right.

It is unlike night.

I wish I could see her now in all her encumbent glory. Tearing through the clouds in a chariot pulled by albino peahens.

You missed your turn. I said Pulltight Road. Where she lives with her dogs and her beautiful preemie baby and her wild iconographic creations.

Pulltight. I said.

My hands have changed. The fingers limber and lengthen.

The Eye Bank has more stock after Independence Day. Why don't you call back after the 4th.

Bear me along your light-bearing paths.

No more boiled peanuts for me. There's that smalltown swerve again. Pass with care.

I don't want to dream the boneman sticking thorns in my arm. I
n that godless oven of a shed he calls an office. A bug got on me
in there I didn't recognize.

This oppressive little college has 23,000 acres. And that was
a wild turkey running across the campus. When we stop in
Admissions and ask for a catalog, we have to fill out a form,
and they indicate they will mail us one. Mutual paranoia floods
the senses.

Let's blow. I dare you to go in the bathroom in the student
union with this neon magic marker and write: Bite me you
big-balled boogie man.

Scatters Pool Hall. Let's go to a filling station and put on long
pants. Have ourselves an Icehouse.

It is unlike night.

He wanted to learn to play the piano by sitting on the brailled
score. It makes sense, playing with one hand; brailling with the
other is pretty inconvenient.

Just the sentence is chilling. I am a painter. I was a painter. I
once was a painter. And now I see. Not. The comfort of her
mother's white piano. The sweating silver vase with sunflowers.

Sunflower blindness.

Ghost hair nestled in streamers across the strings.

In the ceaselessly decomposing smoke of a pool hall. Seven
green tables are racked under seven naked bulbs. The jukebox
in the din calls the man a blanketyblankblank. If not the exact
words the exact tenor. The plate glass casts glimpses of
everything that has ever happened. The genesis of direction
breaks and scatters.

The poor, miserable, garishly rich woman. Like fuchsia.
Wanting the reticence of crepe myrtle. Which is pitched higher
crepe or crape. If I had them, they'd be in the backyard, they'd
be white. Immense, reticent, white bushes.

Hog Waste Lagoon is overflowing. *From the west down to the east.*

Want an onion. They're Vidalias. Now do you know where we are.

Did you ask the taxidermist about the eyes. Do you have to be
an ocularist as well. Was she the only woman in her class in
taxidermy school.

The ocularist has to build and design the eye, stain it; the iris
color, the veins and scleral tint must be perfect. Not a near match.
Only the wearer knows for sure.

Shit. I burned the shit out of my shit-eating tongue.

I said I had a mean streak. Whom do you meet in the mirror.

When we get to Paradise Garden let's call home. May the light
be optimal. Overcast. There is so much glass there.

God is Louise. Is that what it says.

I couldn't miss a mirror. I'd miss everything else. The whole
chlorophylled sward.

Shelled butterbeans. The sign by itself makes me hungry. But
who cooks beans in a motel. Unless one lived there.

The memory jug you bought. Did you hear a voice from within.

The name on the stone was Patience Fish. Isn't that nice. Near
Cloud's Fly Shop.

The taxidermist. Did you say her name was Louise. Vomited the
first three weeks.

They are strictly into columns. Our fingertips do not touch if we
both stand here. Why it would take at least three long-armed men
to encircle one. Ionic. Check the volutes.

The Roman who sold the memory jug

assured it were not stolen

from a grave. Near thrown

to the ground under the power.

At the moment of discovery.

The mouth of the jug remained

open and cool. As a well. A watery

sound emanated from within.

Though his sight were good then.

He were lost. Off Pulltight Road.

Ten years or more ago. The

sky, convict grey. Optimal.

For photographing. Responsive

to his surroundings. All matter

apprehended as one. Immanent.

Yet led there so separate.

Positioned parallel to and apart.

He parked the car. Shouldered

his tripod and walked around.

His last landscapes. Uninhibited

by temporality and men.

Because of the embedded bifocals,

baby spoon, mirror shards…

The jug shone on him.

Shewed itself. Chose him.

By the same gift of clarity

he owned the first wristwatch

in Rome, Georgia.

Thrasher said he had to share with us what was written on
the bathroom wall: Bite me you big-balled boogie man. Maybe he
meant b-a-l-d.

Like the man who made whirligigs who said his daddy taught
him to shoot rabbits in the rocks. Maybe he meant actual rocks.

Why would anyone choose the absence of chlorophyll. Is orange
really your favorite color. Don't you just love a trumpet vine.

And if thy left eye offend thee pluck it out.

I don't know about a chicken, but a cat will eat a cast-off eye.
Chicken love. Cat eyes (come shining).

Morning glories. What's yours.

A chicken will eat anything. I have heard they stack the crates
eight-high, and feed only the birds on top. A fact is a fact. Lore
is lore. And drunk is drunk.

At present the white elephant is extinct. That's right, she said,
they might come back. O go on.

O the chicken on the bottom. He would moan when we tailgated
a Tyson truck.

He did not go see his brother in the hospital. He was ashamed
of his lesions.

What's that spot on the wall. His brother said at last. That's
god's hand said his mother who could not see the spot. Coming
to take you home.

God is Louise.

Moss flew to the clotheslines on Ann Street on silver operatic wings.

His father took off work for two weeks. Without pay of course.
And slept in the hospital bed with his 32-year-old son. Dad, I love you
a bushel and a peck and a hug around the neck. That's child's talk.
The father, 61, said.

Tears sheeting his cheeks. That's tenderness.

Do you like lamb germs, he asked his father. Lamb germs? I
guess so son. I never thought about them before.

What's that spot on the wall.

Everybody in their bed needs love. Body love. Bible love.
Blood love.

"Never avert your eyes." (Kurosawa)

"By the rays of Light I understand its least parts, and those as well
successive in the same lines as contemporary in several lines." Tell it (Sir Isaac).

There. That saucer of light.

That's god's light son.

If I were born long long ago would you give me a zoetrope. It would be a
most beloved toy.

He would take the doorknob into his study with him.

Don't touch that dial.

Long ago they called it a bleeding heart. She said from her porch. When
I asked. Hers grew as tall as the lamppost. They call it something else nowadays.

Hannah she calls the sun.

Love it Leave it Love it Leave it Love it Leave it Love it
Leave it Lo

Just stay quiet. Listen awhile. The white piano misses us. The white
dog dreaming under the white bench is catching up with the cottontail.

The Mexicans say, not the man in the moon, but the rabbit strumming
his *guitara*. Wonder what they say in Seoul.

Or in Poetry.

When you go to pee, shut your eyes and grab a tree.

In the living room of a saint. Watching television. With an ice-cream headache. Assume lotus position. A documentary in black and white. Of young men and women with AIDS. Preparing to die. Communicating, wanting above all to be able to communicate, the alpha and omega of all things unfamiliar to us: Visions ringed with seas. The hatching of supernovae. Deep music. Balanced between two tones. July by lotuslight. Poetry at a standstill.

Trusting in the Haptic Sense

This has to be a watermelon.

This my hand, this yours.

This the heel of a foot. Nay, a potato, it's a potato, Baby.

That's a shovel.

That's a dress shoe.

The radio. The King James. Roses

they're not real though.

This is my number one guitar.

I bought it in downtown Macon in 19 and 42.

These are your prize peahens, I know them. Where's Becky at.

Between the *a* and the *t*.

Chicken hearts are good for the eyes. Full of zinc.

Mmmhmm.

Vitamin A help your retinas adjust.

Carrots and tomatoes are good, spinach, sweet potatoes, pumpkin.

Mmmhmm. Come sit alongside me

on this plasticky couch.

Let me put my arm up here.

Let me rove over to my good side now.

Let me see how large you are.

Let me squeeze your upper knee.

Let me inspect this velvety damp stuff. Unhuh.

Come my sultry refulgence,

can you name the four areas of surrender.

I do believe I smell

a rooster cooking. Mmmhmm.

That's how I know my young feeling has been restored to me.

Listen to that blind man say he smell a rooster cooking.

Pattycake lives here. She's one of the Jumping Foxes, the Double-Dutch Champs. Can you take her picture while we're here. I'll look for the funeral of a stranger to attend.

He's not rambling is he.

The end of the silver queen. I've got to have me one more cob before I croak.

Odontokeratoprosthesis: a tooth for an eye. A gruesome procedure, but not a bad trade.

The donor of course must not have syphilis. Why don't you call back after the 4th.

At one time Milledgeville was a bird sanctuary.

The worst is not so long as we can say, "This is the worst." Isn't that the truth. Deepstep now baby deepstep. Bear me along your light-bearing paths. Come shining.

I'm not long on ruins, but I wanted to stop. The walls of the church were intact. The chairs and pews were wrecked. But the baptismal font, with seven descending steps, I had never seen one emptied out. Trumpet vine in profusion over every brick and windowpane.

Mystery, mystery and a curse.

The watery grave. Take the boneman's hand.

Is that your cane slashing through the grass.

Deepstep come shining.

If I shell those beans for you, will you cook a mess for me. There goes Hannah behind that cloudlet.

> They hung in there when I was broke and sorry.
> They hung in there when I was mean and nasty.
> They hung in there when I was drunk and strung out.
> They hung on in.

After the iridectomy
the slow recognition of forms

A shirt on the floor looked like
the mouth of a well

Spots on a horse
horrible holes in its side

The sun in the tree
green hill of crystals

Moon over Milledgeville
only a story

Saucer of light on the wall
the hand of god

Especially in this town. Everybody needs love. House love. Dishes love. Moth-on-the-screendoor love, spot-on-the-wall love. That's god's hand. Known as the persistence of vision, the eyes' ability to perceive a series of still images as continuous motion.

Don't those totems scare you, Thrasher.

Hell, nothing scares me but real life. Bite me you big-balled boogie man.

What do you call those snakes with legs you make. I call them river dogs. I get the wood off the river. So I call them river dogs.

Ghosts have hair you know. It flies in on silver operatic wings.

I hope he has not mutilated himself. Maybe he meant b-a-l-d.

She had painted her trailer skirt to read: COMING SOON Jesus Christ in All His Glory. It's her trailer skirt, she can say what she likes. What she feels. What she believes. What she sees (Coming Soon).

Paint what you see. Undifferentiated dark. It is unlike night.

In the kingdom of cling peaches, fireworks, red ants.

Odontokeratoprosthesis. Literally a tooth for an eye. A gruesome procedure. I won't go into it. But when the painter went to Barcelona for the operation the surgeon took the sutures out of his lids and said, Too late. You will never see.

The lids sewn shut like pockets on a new jacket. You must smell your way to Dover.

The ruin under the lids. Voices emanating from the emptiness. The memory jug's ancestors.

I am sorry. I mean for no one to come to such harm. But vulnerability in a man. I find it very appealing. Forgive me. I do not mean to intrude. Whereas cowardice is commonplace. Among men. Vulnerability it's a rarity.

Early every evening she sits on the steps of her trailer. The

dirt yard raked. Caterpillar fording the furrows. Mercy,

Louise. If it wasn't hot hot hot. Cornlight. Eyes drink the

color and are refreshed. Images seen but not interpreted.

Thanks to her lovely twin trees the water she drew was cool.

Cool the water she drank from the pump.

Stop at Bulldog's will you for a six-pack of Icehouse.

The cornea does the work. The back wall is the retina.

Just a drop of silver nitrate in the newborn's eyes. It's the law. In case of syphilis. Thus are we treated as thieves in a department store and syphilitics in a hospital. Even the newborn gets *the treatment.*

We live by the etcetera principle.

All the cool people liked the children's humping line dance. All the rest were horrified.

When in Rome…

By the rays of Light I understand its least parts, how my life does not appear in cursive, but in handwrit letters. Crudely executed.

SALVATION. DON'T LEAVE EARTH WITHOUT IT.

Ma'am, are these your glasses.

Here we live and breathe in all the glory of this Vidalia onion. Lengths of pecan trees whipping by. Coming soon. In all his glory. Suddenly I have the feeling of a great victory. A delirious brilliance. Onionlight.

Corner of Hamlet and Bridges. A Jazz Messiah was born here 9/23/26. That's one little step for a man. Seven or eight Giant Steps for mankind. Empty, plate-glass light of Hamlet, North Carolina.

The door locked and the blue room opens only for private parties.

Don't touch that dial.

In the town with the clothesline ordinance the women are bleaching their teeth.

She has Casa Blanca lilies. I covet.

The fiddle contest will take place rain or shine.

Private-party love. By one sixty-watt bulb. And it be blue.
The cool produces an halation. The couple standing under-
neath stir the floor as one. Some modeling on the side of the
face. When directly below the bulb. All other detail dropped
out. The eye gradually grows accustomed to this. The music
circling. Huge and dark. *Eroico furore*. Supremely insane.
Accelerated arpeggios. Unchain a cruel streak. Breath. Nerve.
Mind. Pain. Teeming tonal centres. D-state. Nocturnal emission
of sperm. Corner of Hamlet and Bridges. And in the last year.
They say he did. See angels. A synergism of cancer and dwelling
in musical extremis.

Get the hell out of here. Can't you see I'm not dressed. Can't you see. Anything.

If it's too hot or too cold or there's too much nitrogen in the dirt tomatoes won't set. How can I look my old daddy in the face and say I can no longer bring a tomato to set.

Lights out, Hon.

During which, the hatching of supernovae. Acres and acres of them.

Corner of Hamlet and Bridges. Did you say he met a woman there that went by Louise?

My hands have changed. Deepstep baby. It's zero visibility. And the fish aren't biting.

I left my chicory-blue swimsuit in Augusta. Where you left the grey hair diffuser. When you asked your mother when her red hair began to grey. She looked at you like you were crazy, How the hell should I know. The first few she plucked; thereafter, her purses were never without foils of henna.

The light is antebellum. Ionian man. Everybody inhale.

I had an operation on my back, between my shoulder blades. A potato-sized stone was set in. I recognize the ones who have had this operation.

No. Pattycake was Pie's husband. He brought her a sack of robins.

Look-alikes fall in love.

My family loves cream corn.

Her scarves were made from the whiskers of wild Himalayan goats. He fell into her sensorium. There was nothing left for me to do but fold.

If I offer a breakfast of peasant bread and milk. If I practice the poetry of secession. If I tell you my words are not feathered.

I left my chicory-blue swimsuit back at the motel where the baseball team cannonballed us out of the pool. They won the first day because they played smart ball. The next day they lost because they stayed up all night and didn't play smart ball. When asked his position, the bucktooth said he rode the pines.

Some ghost hair flew into the room and collapsed over the lampshade.

He was willing to let the paintings he destroyed stand for him. His despair absented him from the chlorophylled world.

Weird planets of the eyeballs orbiting the abyss.

He feels only a certain tightness about the eyes.

Push his nose. He'll let you off on whatever floor you want.

.

God bless the Lumière brothers. Lead us, guide us. We are crossing over one by one.

Did you see that. Sorry. It was one of those followers of what's-his-face that throw birds in cars at stoplights.

I don't like B&Bs. I don't like to talk to the host. Let's go to an Indian-owned-and-operated place. A Jenny Lind Motel. Pay up and shut up. Cable, a/c, pool, and no bedbugs.

Don't park in the shade on my account.

OK. One B&B. Colonel Yancy's. The young, urban, African-American professional in the Colonel's eyelet-canopied bed, sent down from Charlotte to set up a branch bank. Why do you think he had a vault in his hall. He didn't trust banks. Forget female African-American bankers. Take a deepstep, Colonel. Your time is done gone.

Love it Leave it Love it Leave it Love it Leave it Love it Love it Lea

The donor of course must not have syphilis.

Doctor S.L. Bigger, captured by the Bedouins, kept a pet antelope, blind in one eye. He took out a fresh-killed antelope's eye, and put it in his pet's head, and the pet saw whole again.

My tomatoes are as tall as this post. And nary a tomato on them. Do you think I am under a curse.

He's not out rambling is he.

She wanted to buy the stuffed bobcat in the antique store, but the owner said it was his logo.

A wild turkey running across the road right on the campus. 23,000 acres. A kingdom. I wouldn't go to school there for love or money.

And if thy right eye offend thee pluck it out.

Cold eyes are bad to eat.

These gourds are kindly expensive. But would you wont anythang that wasn't.

I see your point.

As a child I was a kleptomaniac. But I'm a very nice person now. I wouldn't take a napkin without my doctor's permission.

When the lightning hit the mute swan. In all her glory. The students were traumatized. They were in the refectory overlooking the lake. When the lightning hit the mute swan. In all her glory. She exploded. Her five cygnets sizzled on the surface.

There will be no more night.

When I lay my hand on the live oak I wondered how many pencils would it yield. Pencils of days and of hips and lilies. Pencils of Novocain and commotion.

That self-conscious Southern poetry, preposterous as a wedding dress.

The old washing machine Clyde uses to make her papier-mâché from the *Atlanta Constitution*. Finally broke. She'll never find parts.

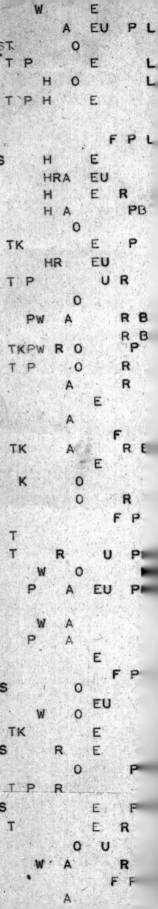

When the aim is to feel wholeness itself. She laid her hand on the deeply furrowed bark, groping for the area of darkest color. The trunks would be painted with a palette. Solids would develop from the center outward. Avoiding any kind of line. The body pressed against the trunk until she were certain of being extinguished by the darkness. One achieves a concealed drawing. Which is most like night.

The Colonel's curtains whiten in unelaborating rays. His clawfoot tubs. Big-tub love.

What's that spot on the wall. That light saucer.

She wanted to fall to her knees under petals of snow. In a stark white dormitory. Twelve white cakes would be brought to a cloth-draped table by twelve starched women. All of this mystery, mystery, mystery.

If I can't coax a twelve-foot tomato plant to yield one juicy mouthful. I must be under a curse.

What if we stay here long enough to attend a stranger's funeral. I like this spot.

And when the sudarium was removed, wrap by wrap…
Too late the doctor said. You will never see.

Look-alikes fall in love. Unless…

O my irises. My irises. O the sidewalls of my breasts.

It reminds me of my back life. If I had stayed I would have married the no-count. He couldn't help it. He had no luck. They took his luck and tied it to a rabbit's neck.

Trailer living was appealing when I was seventeen.

We need a preponderance of love.

Ride. Eat. Sleep. It said on his T-shirt.

The darkness will eat you. They say in Bosnia.

The LED emits the following diode: This is the time to see and to feel WHOLES.

Color. Degree of brightness. Saturation: Hue. Value. Chroma. He had a passion for nomenclature.

Ride. Eat. Sleep

Oncet   after a heavy rain

he come back   at daybreak

threw down a few dollars and cents

alongside a set   of pretty glass eyes

into a little dish on the dresser

flopped crosswise on the bed and slept

I started to write   I feel lost here

and I'm going to go home   Oncet

I clave to him   like fog but the bus

at Dahlonega   wasn't waiting for me

to go through the old lucubrations

and Brother Veal of Deepstep nor was I

Could I have a touch of your vitreous humor.

What does she look like, the handsome young blind man asked his pretty, freckled girl at the festival.

She has black hair. Strange, he said. I pictured her blond.

The rain would let up and then it would start up. Some brought umbrellas. Some turned garbage bags into ponchos.

The refrain to the rain would be a movement up and down the clefs of light.

The boats in the bay took in the festival from the water.

Blur in. Blur out.

The darkness will eat you.

A bullet don't have nobody's name on it.

HAIR TODAY. GONE TOMORROW. (sign at the electrolysis center) Dontouchmymustache. That's all the Japanese I can say.

They didn't have a metal detector. So you know folks were packing. Club Paradise. Saturday night. Bowlegs Miller led the house band.

> What are you going to do when our lamps are gone out.
> What are you going to do.
> What are you going to do when you come to the crossroad.

Everybody in this clinic needs love. A preponderance of love.

The eye is an image-catching device. On this much we are agreed.

They dropped silver nitrate in my new baby's eyes. According to law. A poisonous colorless crystalline compound. Used in manufacturing photographic film, silvering mirrors, dyeing hair, plating silver, and in medicine as a cautery and antiseptic.

First the light sinks to shadows. The shadows become
flooded with broad washes of dark. Watch. As the dark comes
entirely into its own. Watch. The light being eaten. Devoured.
Sonorous certainty of the dark. What sets the hangers in a
closet singing in unison. The light murdered, that the truth
become apparent.

```
ST  P  H              F  P
ST  P  H              F  P
    T  P           EU  R

        HR       EU
    S                EU  PB
      T           .O
      S       H  A
                   O
                              F  P
      T
      S       H  A
                   O
            PW                      B
      T  P  HRAO

              W
            PW  R  O
              W     A          R  B

                              F
    TK          A              R  B
                              F  P
              W     A          R  B
                              F  P
                    A
    TK          A              R  E
      K             O              P
                         E      PE
    T                   EU  R
          HR        EU
    T  P  H
    T               O
                    O              PE
                              F  P
            W     A            R  E
                              F  P

    T
          HR      EU
                              E
                      E
                      E      PE
                         F  P
    TX                E
    S         R  O    U  R
                         F  R
    S             A
    T  P  H  O          R
                   U
```

Is that why the newborn looks like an alien. Or did the grey
ones inseminate me. Do the grey ones know I am not a proper specimen.

God is Louise. Louise moves in mysterious ways. Coming soon.

Are we not fearfully and wonderfully made.

Tell those Lumière brothers, I appreciate everthang they done.

If I tell you it's a ten-dollar bill how are you going to know the
difference if it's a one. If I tell the house painter, eggshell white, how
do I know she won't paint it orange. Trumpet-flower orange.

Ride. Eat. Sleep. Where on earth will we go next. What will we
do when the money is gone. What're you going to do when your lamp's
gone down. Tuck your shirttail in.

Word spreads.

The first menses in the dark days, winter. Born blind, early onset.

Lead me to the river with your mirror.
Unwrap the sudarium from my face.
Lead me, guide me, to the faraway deep down. Then steal away
in alligatorlight.

Which is brighter g-r-a-y or g-r-e-y. Which is pitched higher.

How do I look. I have forgotten. Deepstep come shining.

For I am the cipher in her story in which she robbed his grave
of its voice and appears herself as an old angel. All that is there is the
ghost of his breath. The hair of his ghost got caught up in my lines.
In the night it flew here. It is the hair that makes it so mysterious.

O your giant TV. Do you watch much. What is there to watch.
This is the time to see and to feel WHOLES.

Blur in. Blur out.

Were we not fearfully and wonderfully made.

I always did have a spidery hand. You know what it says.

Is this the hand that will lead me to the river. Lead me along your light-bearing paths. Do you leave the mirror in the river.

We were young. We was happy. Were we not. Happy. Young. Wasn't we.

The eye is a mere mechanical instrument.

Leaning over the white piano, breathing in her petals. The mute swan exploded. With the students looking on. In all her glory.

A white house among the white hydrangea trees.

Now that is an Arkansas toe sticking out from that sheet if I ever saw one.

She wears me out. Doesn't she you. Can't she play anything else.

Is this where he swapped a motorcycle that didn't work for a pinball machine that didn't work.

It is not that we live in a world of colored objects but that surfaces reflect a certain portion of the light hitting them. It's all whiteness. Here, in Ultima Thule.

The noise of the retina as you get older.

Known by her neighbors to garden by flashlight. Sometimes, she said, the darkness creeps up on me.

Whenever I see a walk-ins-welcome sign I want to walk on in. Whenever I see a we-reserve-the-right-to-refuse-service-to-anyone sign I want to shake my white panties at the boss.

Suddenly I have the feeling of a great victory.

Then there's the no-shoe-no-shirt-no-service; the you-break-it-you-pay-for-it. And the employees-must-pluck-out-an-eye-before-returning-to-work.

Blur in. Blur out. Just a hypothetical blind woman brought
out of completest dark. Looking at a face. She will know it
belongs to Pattycake if Pattycake laughs. Counting trees by
the shadow of their trunk. Looking at something blue. That's
the river. Something green. That's the grass. Something else
blue. That's sky. Stood mutely in front of a lone tree. Sees
only the spaces in between. That's the tree with the lights
in it. Tuck your shirttail in. Now this. Is my very own hand.
I always did have a spidery hand.

After he lost his sight, he could discriminate colors by their vibration. He was thrown to the ground under the power.

The water here, black marble. The grass, army-surplus green.

Poking around in the woods with a gun. Poke around in the house with a book. Poke around. Poke around.

They bleach their teeth those women.

Are those Casa Blanca lilies. I covet.

We lunch on Onion River. Stop by Cloud's Fly Shop.

Fiddle contest tomorrow rain or shine.

Get the hell out of here, can't you see I'm not dressed. Can't you see I'm depressed.

I see. I see.

Please don't put your feet on the chairs, it said in the eye doctor's office. Please don't spit on the floor, it said in my father's courtroom.

Her Aunt Flo said she hadn't had any in so long she'd done growed back together.

Are you still working on that drink.

Cold pop. Free air. Sold here.

We never close. Every nickel counts. Just ask Big Sam. He suctioned every nickel from every small town pocket and he sewed it under his lids, a veritable sheik from Arkansas.

He put a pillow over her mother's head and shot her. The white piano shivered in the corner like a boy with an orchid.

That was a helluva note.

After the iridectomy
she fell to the ground under the power

The boxwoods that lined the road
were walking with her

She could touch the willow wands on the other side of Little

Lynches River

She smudged the passage she had once felt

She was fearful of putting a morsel of cake
in her mouth

She thought it too large to enter in

A pool of shade appeared bottomless

The contours of a man were horrible to her
those of the family dog were bearable

A pool of shade appeared bottomless

Two white horses side by side. Going to take her on her farewell ride.

Ain't it hawd.

Half-fare, blind, mmhmm.

Nothing in the world beats time.

She said her sister was more like Aunt Flo everyday. Big blond Aunt Flora with the smutty mouth who said she hadn't had any in so long it'd done growed back together.

In the gated communities the women are bleaching their teeth.

Shielding her eyes among her Casa Blanca lilies with a tad of a hangover she offers spiderweb to staunch his paper cut.

Cloud's Fly Shop in spitting distance.

Fiddle contest rain or shine, declares the flyer on the creosote pole.

I see. I see.

Don't you just hate it when your gown catches between your buttocks.

Don't you just hate it when the waiter says, Are you still working on that drink.

Poke around. Poke around. Can't you see I'm depressed. Welcome to my sensorium. You can touch, but you cannot lie.

You must know the Veals of Deepstep.

Mother's neighbor passes on her mower, riding (*sic*) her Clancy novel.

She suffers from what Wittgenstein called aspect blindness. Is it a rabbit. Nay, it's a swan, a swan.

Branches drop without warning. Clouds accumulate around

a kind of idea akin to sonic weight. Progressive darkness.

250 miles offshore with winds at 105 MPH, Bertha turns

inland. Multitudes of windows crossed with masking tape.

Evacuation mandatory in the low-lying areas. Contrasts

annihilated. Concealing loneliness and fear. As when the lens

opening is too small. Taken too late. Or too early. Uncharacteristic

silence loading the car. Worry over maundering. Hunger over

worry. Tranquilized with a private jukebox in Formicalight.

Endless refills. Pigs-in-the-blanket-and-grits-on-the-side time.

Beats the bejesus out of Bertha's maw. Now do you know where

you are. My over-air-conditioned-and-caffeinated love.

Come shining. I have you in hand, Deepstep.

That's Junebug's place. It's a mess. He was way old a long time before I ever was born. His daddy was a Senator. Lived at Twelve Oaks. Tornado pulled up all twelve and tossed them in the fields like drinking straws. Without the oaks it looks like an asylum. For the criminally insane.

She was my friendgirl for three years. We were thick. Then she ran off and got married. Her mother and I sat on the scratchy plaid sofa crying. Too young. Too young.

> She hung on in when they runover his dog.
> She hung on in when he caught his hand in the trolling motor.
> She hung on in when he starting talking out of his head.
> She hung on in when he flunked the polygraph.
> She hung on in.

Come on, Hon. If you come undone. I come undone. You take two eggs over or one.

Sixteen. The white piano shivered in the dark like a boy with an orchid.

He set fire to his birthday present, the white angora sweater, in the judge's driveway. Because she wouldn't go all the way.

I see, I see.

The Veals of Deepstep. They are very prominent.

Bright light flooded in horizontally from the left.

It fell obliquely on her body, which subtly responded to the interruption.

If Louise is god can her evanescence be fixed.

The amount of sunlight striking each one of her pearls.

Don't disabuse her, the grass widow of her aura of originality *with her pearls and her amphetamines.*

The scrape of chairs on a stone floor. A sack of birds escaped in the house. Fleshy, velvety dampness. Panic. Time lapse. Silence. That they think only of sight while they chew. Slowly the hand unwraps the bandages. Until the night shuts like a door. And the light slams from his face. Interrupting the flow of stimuli. It is all whiteness, he says, even this sightlessness.

Besides, even a rat can strike a match.

The politics are so deep. Ceaselessly, yes ceaselessly.

The moon is vagrant and the prey senses the predator's warm breath; the hale sleep naked atop the sheet.

How Walt's saintly white beard was reported to attract butterflies.

Her late husband was a poet. He had some beautiful thoughts. He published in *Ideal* and other places. He had all kinds of rhyme schemes and everything. So meticulous. Sometimes. It would make you think.

That's right. An ordinary rat can scratch a match, and burn a good house down to the ground.

Forms nearest the eye appeared blurred. We have been separated by a chair. The blind man taught my uncle to cane in an afternoon. He found the chair in Mamo's attic. It took him two weeks. And then his wife did the stenciling.

Gold leaf is obtainable in small booklets. But it'll cost you.

Stole a watermelon oncet. Stole some sugar.

> Remember me to all of them. Bite everybody on the lips for me. Remember me forever.
> *Recuérdame siempre.* It says on the blade of the knife he hung from a string. The tip of it twirling over his pillow while he dreamed. How that man loved to dream.

Salvation. Don't leave earth without it. Or your glasses. There is so much to see.

Pattycake was Pie's husband.

Caution. Deep step.

Photo graphein of an old plaid couch in a field as its sunken cushions emptied of bodies and filled with leaves, then snow, then rain; then the seams split and the batting bubbled out for the birds and squirrels to carry off by the beak- and clawful.

Don't touch that dial. Here's the rest of the story: These
three ladies they had been into all manner of wrongdoing.
They were wearing the evil one's varsity jacket. They were
hot for god and they were on fire. That night they were thrown
to the ground under the power. That night the glory cloud
filled the church. The prayer line stayed open that night. A
real hard light, sharp, cold as a nail, split right through the
boards. Angels went to banging around in the rafters like barn
swallows. We'll pick up at the next chapter, dearly beloveds…

He hogged the bed.
She hogged the covers.
He hogged the meat.
She hogged the conversation.

Hush, hogs, hush.

She hung on in. *With her pearls and her amphetamines.*

A pencil of rays was all that he could make out. He would be shewn the rest by touch.

Images may be either real or virtual.

Hearing is the last sense to go.

Did you ask Thrasher if that was a lapdog in his freezer.

I thought you were taking pictures of the Double-Dutch Champs.

The funeral was postponed until tomorrow.

Stay here with me. If you don't mind the dark. We can talk until the tape runs out. It has the aura of an original.

If Louise is the answer what is the question. Are we stuck here or what. Anyway, the singing's not helping much.

Who's there. Is that you, Deep Step.

O my irises. My irises. And the sidewalls of my breasts.

See this hand. See this. Come shining.
The hand that peeled the bark from my birches.
The hand that stirred the pencil of my life.
That took a belt to my hebetude.
The hand that explored my body cavities, hand of the
         selenographer, mapper of lost roads.
That picked my bones (white).
The hand that anticipated everything. While the fishermen
         of Borneo were stealing telephone booths.
That took me in deep (step by step).
That prepared my colors.
Then picked my brain (clean).
The hand that pulled my last Vidalia out of the garden and
         ate it dirt, bulb, and green.
That spread itself out on my window.
Eidolon of light (even as it decomposes).
Then made known to me the deep blindness of coitus and
         denied me a ladder to see out.

We can't send this message   no positive way

hallelujah   glory to ya   they call it the hump

day   if you can get over the hump you've got it

made   position yourself to hear

somewhere around the 14th verse   we need

an elevator   to help us look in the present

to help us visualize the future   thank you

for your call   can't you see   not of this

world   who has no way   somebody say   what is

a leader   who knows the way   goes the way

shows the way   just in case

somebody doesn't know   what I'm talking

about   the commission to be a friend

to the lost people   this goes out to the air

the sweet barbecue of night   I want to

magnify   praise is the gate   to enter in

sit down   I said please sit down   the more

you praise the clearer the mind becomes   I said I

love you   I adore you   I called didn't I   praise is

the gate   to enter in   we need an elevator   to

take our lost friends up   to the auditorium

of light   didn't I call   O world world world

I but stumbled when I saw   praise is the gate

to enter   plenty of parking   come early

to get a good seat

Look for a clear object (Case #33)

Don't need a magnifying glass

To make the feelings seen

Softly unwrap bandages

Unlike paper torn off a wall

Place yourself inside the damage

Lights approaching top speed

Blur in, blur out

A need for linear relief

Everything going awful fast

Trees agitated by wind

Keep the setting simple

A bowl of sugar on a table

Separated by a chair

Not an inkling what it means

Urge to withdraw

Pull the ladder up after

In the hither world I lead you willingly along the light-bearing paths. In the hither world I offer a once-and-for-all thing, opaque and revelatory, ceaselessly burning. Anyone who has ever been through a fire knows how devastating it can be. The furniture lost, books collected over thirty years, the mother's white piano. I was there. I know.

Stimulants, Poultices, Goads

Opticks or a Treatise of the Reflections, Refractions, Inflections and Colours of Light by Sir Isaac Newton; Forrest Gander, Akira Kurosawa, *Smoke*, Bone Man, Snake Man, Norman Schwarzkopf, James Agee, *Georgia: The WPA Guide to Its Towns and Countryside*, Farmer's Almanac; WBY, the Beatles, James Dickey, Frank Stanford, Holy Bible; *The Book of Common Prayer*; *Eclipse: A Nightmare* by Hughes DeMontalembert; Bob Dylan, Flannery O'Connor, Roger Dorset, the Lumière brothers, Margaret Vittitow, Carolyn Merritt, John Coltrane, Peter Gurnis, Shelby Morgan, Deborah Luster, *Encyclopædia Britannica*; Paradise Garden, Stephen Beard, Stephen Engstrom, Bill Smart, Matthew 5:27–30, *King Lear*; *The Art of Cézanne* by Kurt Badt; *Blake* by Peter Ackroyd; *It Came* from Memphis by Robert Gordon; Aunt Mildred, Paul Harvey, *A Pair of Blue Eyes* by Thomas Hardy; Ft. Lauderdale radio ministry; Vic Chesnutt's *Is the Actor Happy*; *Vision and Design* by Roger Fry; *Space and Sight* by M. von Seden; *Howard Finster: Man of Visions* by J.F. Turner; station WLLL; *The Freedom Principle: Jazz after 1958* by John Litweiler; Reverend Pearly Brown, Anne Truitt, *Mental Healers* by Stefan Zweig; Alyce Collins Wright, court reporter (retired); Virginia Center for the Creative Arts and its artist fellows in the summer of 1996.

for Alyce Collins Wright
Court Reporter for 11th Chancery District of Arkansas
1961–1975

for Fern Raulston Nicholson
Court Reporter for 14th Judicial Circuit of Arkansas
1961–1975

from ONE BIG SELF

Prisoners of Louisiana (2002)

Count your fingers
Count your toes
Count your nose holes
Count your blessings
Count your stars (lucky or not)
Count your loose change
Count the miles to the state line
Count cars at the crossing
Count the ticks you pulled off the dog
Count your shells
Count the points on the antlers
Count the newjack's keys
Count the beds you've got to let
Count your cards; cut them again

My Dear Conflicted Reader,

If you will grant me that most of us have an equivocal nature, and that when we waken we have not made up our minds which direction we're headed; so that—you might see a man driving to work in a perfume- and dye-free shirt, and a woman with an overdone tan hold up an orange flag in one hand, a Virginia Slim in the other—as if this were their predestination. Grant me that both of them were likely contemplating a different scheme of things. WHERE DO YOU WANT TO SPEND ETERNITY the church marquee demands on the way to my boy's school, SMOKING OR NON-SMOKING. I admit I had not thought of where or which direction in exactly those terms. The radio ministry says g-o-d has a wrong-answer button and we are all waiting for it to go off…

The septuagenarian murderer knits nonstop

One way to wear out the clock

In Tickfaw miracles occur

This weekend: the thirteenth annual Cajun joke contest

They will/will not be sending the former governor to Big Gola

I pinch a cigarette and stare at Rachel's wrist scars

By their color they are recent

That the eye not be drawn in

I suggest all courage is artificial

Her sister did not fail

Noses amuse us and hers not less so

Short   fair   smart   butch
    utterly unsure of herself

Whichever you see as sadder

A jukebox or a coffin

A woman's hand will close your eyes

On the surface she is receptive

I wear the lenses of my time

Some run to type, but I am not qualified

Hectored by questions that have to do with The Forms of Harm,
    The Nature of the Beast, Mercy, etc.

Last seen yesterday morning in a one-piece swimsuit

The popular sixteen-year-old is 5'7", 127 lbs.

The K-9 unit given her long white prom gloves, her pillowcase

Do you wish to save these changes
     yes   no   never mind

The ants of Tickfaw pour onto the bark
    in the form of a cross

A random book skimmed from the women's shelf

In which an undine-like maiden
    is espied feeding white daisies to a bear

Something on anarcho-syndicalism wasn't really expected

    poetry   time   space   death

Church marquee: AFTER GOOD FRIDAY COMES EASTER
    GOD ALWAYS WINS

Drive-in marquee: LENTEN SPECIAL
    POBOYS   FRIES   DRINK

The men pretty much all have ripped chests

Knitting wasn't really expected

Sign on the weight machine: PUSH TO FAILURE

She is so sweet you wouldn't believe she had did
    all the things they say she did

That one, she's got a gaggle of tricks up her you-know-what

Drawn on a wall in solitary by a young one
    mom   love   god

    before he had a face on him

Don't blink don't miss nothing: It's *your* furlough

The Asian lady beetle won't reproduce indoors

The missing girl's father is a probation officer

Do you want to download this
    Now   Later   No Comment

Solitary confinement, Mr. Abbott wrote,
    can alter the ontological makeup of a stone

Mr. Abbott was state-raised, he knows

Zero % financing and drive-through daiquiris

Baggies of hair and nail clippings entered in

You can bet your nickels

The former 4-term governor will be well-lawyered

What is *your problem*

The tier walker checks on the precariously living

Photographed him with a boner

That's not my pencil, is it

It is a stock dog, the state dog, Catahoula
    with the rain-blue eyes

Church marquee: LET'S MEET AT MY HOUSE BEFORE THE GAME

Lead (kindly) light   Enter (softly) evil

Dear Virtual Lifer,

This is strictly a what-if proposition:
What if I were to trade my manumission for your incarceration. If only for a day.
At the end of which the shoes must be left at the main gate to be filled by their
original occupants. There is no point and we will not shrink from it. There is
only this day to reinvent everything and lose it all over again. Nothing will be
settled or made easy.

If you were me:
If you wanted blueberries you could have a big bowl. Two dozen bushes right on
your hill. And thornless raspberries at the bottom. Walk barefooted; there's no
glass. If you want to kiss your kid you can. If you want a Porsche, buy it on the
installment plan. You have so many good books you can't begin to count them.
Walk the dog to the bay every living day. The air is salted. Septembers you can
hear the blues jumping before seeing water through the vault in the leaves. Watch
the wren nesting in the sculpture by the shed. Smoke if you feel like it. Or swim.
Call a friend. Or keep perfectly still. The morning's free.

If I were you:
Screw up today, and it's solitary, Sister Woman, the padded dress with the food log
to gnaw upon. This is where you enter the eye of the fart. The air is foul. The dirt
is gumbo. Avoid all physical contact. Come nightfall the bugs will carry you off.
You don't have a clue, do you.

Count your grey hairs
Count your chigger bites
Count your pills
Count the times the phone rings
Count your T cells
Count your mosquito bites
Count the days since your last menses
Count the storm candles
Count your stitches
Count broken bones
Count the flies you killed before noon

MY DEAR AFFLUENT READER,

Welcome to the Pecanland Mall. Sadly, the pecan grove had to be dozed to build it. Home Depot razed another grove. There is just the one grove left and the creeper and the ivy have blunted its sun. The uglification of your landscape is all but concluded. We are driving around the shorn suburb of your intelligence, the photographer and her factotum. Later we'll walk in the shadows of South Grand. They say, in the heyday of natural gas, there were houses with hinges of gold. They say so. We are gaining on the cancerous alley of our death. Which, when all is said or unsaid, done or left undone, shriven or unforgiven, this business of dying, is our most commonly held goal.

Ready or not. 0 exceptions.

Don't ask.

DEAR PRISONER,

    I too love.   Faces.   Hands.   The circumference
Of the oaks.   I confess.   To nothing
You could use.   In a court of law.   I found.
That sickly sweet ambrosia of hope.   Unmendable
Seine of sadness.   Experience taken away.
From you.   I would open.   The mystery
Of your birth.   To you.   I know.   We can
Change.   Knowing.   Full well.   Knowing.
                          It is not enough.
    poetry   time   space   death
I thought.   I could write.   An exculpatory note.
I cannot.   Yes, it is bitter.   Every bit of it, bitter.
The course taken by blood.   All thinking
Deceives us.   Lead (kindly) light.
Notwithstanding this grave.   Your garden.
This cell.   Your dwelling.   Who is unaccountably free.

Count your folding money
Count the times you said you wouldn't go back
Count your debts
Count the roaches when the light comes on
Count your kids after the housefire
Count your cousins on your mother's side
Count your worrisome moles
Count your dead:

DEAR DYING TOWN,

The food is cheap; the squirrels are black; the box factories have all moved offshore; the light reproaches us, and our coffee is watered down, but we have an offer from the Feds to make nerve gas; the tribe is lobbying hard for another casino; the bids are out to attract a nuclear dump; and there's talk of a supermax—

In the descending order of your feelings

Please identify your concerns

P.S.: Remember Susanville, where Restore the Night Sky has become the town cry.

DEAR ERRANT KID,

Remember the almighty finger on the wrong-answer button.

Count the days of summer ahead
Count the years you finished in school
Count the jobs you don't qualify to hold
Count the smokes you've got left
Count the friends you've got on the inside
Count the ones who've already fallen

Why does it take so goddamn long—the burned-up years, the landscape memorized without benefit of wheels, the nearly pretty house, the nearly nice room, uneventful days, implausible schemes on the heels of unpreventable nights; the perpetually pissed-off ones who just wanted to hurt somebody, the incipiently pissed who had to be roused with a broom; the well-meaners who tried to help; the feckless risks; the nearly helpful teacher, the failures that can be achieved without trying; the sick bosses; the wrong beds with the wrong ones, the unheeded infections, all the ugly run-over shoes, the thousand stupid things you wanted (others had them); the carcasses of your young dumb dreams strewn all over the slithering hills…

If you could just say I feel lost here and I'm going to go home now. For where on earth would you buy that ticket. Who would meet you when you got there. By what sign would they know you.

A man seated below the copia of mounted heads at The Mohawk said he came from Old Floyd. In the town center of Old Floyd they had a bell that came from France, and when hunters lost themselves in the forest the bell would be rung so they could find their way out. It was, the man said, his dream to lose himself in the forest and be saved by the bell. Saved by the bell. Get it.

A circle of blackened rocks, vagrant moon, the trees that say Come near; the bull that doesn't care…

I who once fled north slumped over the pew of a family of prominence and came back with my glasses taped at the stem (as a dog returneth to his vomit).

Longing to touch the unguarded earth, touch it while it is still warm.

Recurrent dream of freedom: You are outside. It rains. The water turns you transparent and sexual—like electricity caught in a jar. Suddenly you are wide awake and everything you ever wanted is here. You will never need gloves again, never be out-of-date. Harm or be harmed, take or be taken. You can cry and creature here. So quietly can you die.

Then the images are upside down, inside out. After typing your entire life, you discover your carbons are in backwards. Where there should be darkness, the light is hard on and vice versa. Except for that long blue rag of land. And the white pelicans on Sugar Lake.

Up north with its thirty minutes in the sun, good schools for the moneyed and silent alarms, and south with its petrochemical plants and joblessness. And the children of children, buckets of children, jumping through snatches of smoke, penitentiary bound.

Barred from both and you miss them terribly.

Linked to an experience   a feeling deep down
that won't stop twisting   until the last rivet of grief is secure

All our days are numbered. Not unlike old lumber for a house that's going to
be moved and lived in all over again. Same old blunders on a different hill.

And you, only a number.

Not a fresh fish anymore.

Got a face on you.

Not a part of, apart from.

Cropped out of the picture.

Vice Versa.

Mack trapped a spider
Kept in a pepper jar
He named her Iris
Caught roaches to feed her
He loved Iris
When Iris died
He wrote her a letter

Or:

Or: Animism

We have degenerated into people. – DUO DUO

We are back from the ark, almost.
Is it always this dark?
Who was here first?
Since it is so lush why does everything have that chemistry-set smell?
Is there still time for a crisis?

It rained. Or did it? There is water yet standing.
When in the late afternoon, everything gets hungry.
If my head should fall off, please don't put it in a sack.
Does one start with the face. Save the jam for the end?

The sign said grave-digging two bodies a day,
sixty cents an hour.
How does one decide what to leave for the others?
If the cheese were all that is left
How would that be ascribable to me?
When the light doesn't cover itself up
then will you see the incision of my words?
We are back from the dark, almost.

What is a savannah anyway?
Dogs everywhere are close kin. Like Amish.
Jesus, the Cistercian biology teacher told them, had 23 chromosomes
And was the spitting image of his mother.

Carcass of love, carrion of the wedding feast.
Go ahead, pick my bones
I dreamed I was biting his arm.
I dreamed he was taking me to Nebraska on foot
for our honeymoon. And this was the best I'd felt in a long time.
Those who question the primacy of the phallus
Are surely in for it.

It stopped raining. But made no discernible difference.
The thirst was and will be with us forever.
And after the dogs, the others would come.
First two, then more; in pairs, then more.

And the hewed stones formed a pair as well. Blackened. Fallen.
Perhaps from a monument. A marker for a significant boundary.
Toppled. Here in the savannah.
Because it is beautiful you should not walk alone.
Because it is beautiful you should not go without shoes.
But take a long look. For the rest of nature is nearly morte.
When I think of dying. I think of the ultimate release from fear.
When I think of dying, I get so scared my body refuses to lie down.
There is always time for a crisis.

     Even here, another Fourth, everyone is prey to the heat
and the drums. Cars supplant the beasts.
     Where was he. He said he would be back before the clouds
broke. And the headlights began streaming down County Road.
     Or he would stay until the final minutes before the finale and
the cars became belligerent and began to degenerate into people.
     He knew the ark would not wait.
     He knew they were booked to the rafters.
     He knew we could lose our cheap seats in the reaches
Where the Julliard students stand up reading the scores.

And therefore, we have to wait for the hyenas to get hungry
enough to kill for their supper. Then we will come
with our napkins tucked under our chins
and our cutlery gleaming. Things seem more eternal
elsewhere. Where one eats until one is eaten.
Never eat to be eating.

     There was a sheen on the road soon after we entered
the city limits. The air, splendid, freshly wetted.
     Have you ever attempted to count the storage tanks when you
passed them on the way back. Have you ever reeled
under the magnitude of petroleum's ruin.

The beast involuntarily turns its rack of ribs up for the pack.
He has pulled into the breakdown lane, burning oil.
If these rags are edible, we will live.

I am the last one in the house to go to bed.
Listen. The insects resume where the fireworks left off.
Or, if not, the insects collect at the light
with their silent scores.

Isn't the engine turning over. Almost.

There must be a re-set button for this machine.

Let's be realistic. We are never coming back.

About Things That Might Go On in Infinite Dimensions

Let the tail of the dog lead: a suspicious man is walking west

dressed all in white. Cardinal numbers shall defer to ordinal. A suspicious letter

arrives in an unknown hand. A glass of water is drunk, a candle sputters; something

goes pop. Every unexpected sound shall be investigated.

THE MEDIUM IS FEAR

Cholera persists, even here. Sincerely, Ursa Minor, have you seen my ankh.

A man dressed all in black is walking northbound, his eyes set close together. A fight

breaks out in aisle 13 of Walmart's and someone is masturbating in the reptile section.

The scent on her comb disappears.

LOSS IS THE MESSAGE

An anonymous caller reports: loud music and goat sacrifices on Old Wire Road.

The dog blows its hair. Between scattered showers and a power outage, this and this happened.

A man reports his surveillance camera stolen and a new motherboard installed. Now, get out
of that silly Ghillie suit, before you are taken for a foreigner.

THE MEDIUM IS CLEAR

In heaven, beds are turned down between six and seven; Thursday marks

the deaths of a retired grocer, a homemaker, a retired plumber, and a quality control worker.

Salvation being local, our gradual dissolution huffs into view.

TOIL IS THE MESSAGE

Constant effort is required, a pound of thrust for every pound

of anything else just to hold our own against the forces. Promise me one thing. Promise

you won't go home with Nosferatu, the mothers tell their sixteen-year-olds

amid a flurry of warnings

from COOLING TIME (2005)

ONLY THE CROSSING COUNTS.

It's not how we leave one's life. How go off

the air. You never know, do you. You think you're ready

for anything; then it happens, and you're not. You're really

not. The genesis of an ending, nothing

but a feeling, a slow movement, the dusting

of furniture with a remnant of the revenant's shirt.

Seeing the candles sink in their sockets; we turn

away, yet the music never quits. The fire kisses our face.

O phthisis, O lotharian dead eye, no longer

will you gaze on the baize of the billiard table. No more

shooting butter dishes out of the sky. Scattering light.

Between snatches of poetry and penitence you left

the brumal wood of men and women. Snow drove

the butterflies home. You must know

how it goes, known all along what to expect,

sooner or later…the faded cadence of anonymity.

    Frankly my dear, frankly my dear, frankly

UNTIL WORDS TURN TO MOSS.

This was all roses, here, where an overblown house crowns

the hill, the whole field, roses, all the way to the end;

when the rosarian died, the partition of roses

began. We've come out of nowhere, literally,

nowhere, autumnal towns marked for destruction

by a phantom hand; houses held underwater, every bed

a sunken tub, tools drowned between rows, every keyhole

caulked; clouds hallucinating girls asleep on a wedge

of wedding cake; the white rose, among the greatest of liars,

beginning to show the debilitating effects of fame;

the ever-popular blaze placates a vase; the bad sons

of thunder beating back a strand of light; someone

who knows nothing apart from the rain

standing on a chair in muddy legs; the roses

blown into their cumulonimbi,

and someone whose glove is recovered, a face

that doesn't come clear, a face drawn under an umbrella,

beautiful, charcoal, beautiful, like words

that never get old, the sons of thunder beating

ELATION WASHED OVER OUR ABSENCE TOWARD EVERYTHING IN THE INCREASING DARKNESS.

The soft coloration of his longing in the indifferent

environment has never deserted me.

My husband saving the spermaceti to light

our eyestrings. My husband charting my obsessions

with characteristic cool. Singing sacerdotally

in the shower, my husband intoning every cleft in my skin.

Our syncopated breathing. My husband who flew often

at night as a child. Above the very ground

of our writing (even as power poles were falling

on volvos). My husband equally popular with women

of all ages. His nail parings, his running legs, his scriptoria.

O his ludic hard head. Who cut down

his own hair with a bone-handled knife. His rack

of gorgeous unworn ties. My husband touching

even the insular men; whenever fear bred

its mushrooms under rugs, a cleaning frenzy commenced.

Our bed irrigated with my blood. Watching me burn

from within; tendering his cross pen. O predominantly

white guilt. Whenever it rained

IN OUR ONLY TIME.

"Follow me," the voice, the long, longed-for voice stops

the writing hand. "I have your shoes." Except

for a rotating fan, movement at a minimum. The plan,

if one can call it a plan, is to be in what is known

to some as the perennial present; beginning

with a few sentences written in a kitchen while others

cling to their own images in twisted sheets of heat.

A napkin floats from a counter in lieu of a letter. Portals

of the back life part in silence: O verge

of song, O big eyelets of daylight. Leaving milk and bowl

on the table, leaving the house discalced. All this

mystery, mildly erotic. Even if one is terrified

of both death and the color red. Even if a message is sent

each of us in secrecy, no one can make it stay.

Notwithstanding scale—everything has its meaning,

every thing matters; no one a means every one an end

    Approximately forever,

    C.D.

after h.l. hix

LIKE SOMETHING FLYING
BACKWARDS

LIKE SOMETHING FLYING BACKWARDS

When a word here and there was starting to escape.

There is some hope that she may yet.

Even by herself could work herself into a fit.

Often thought of death in daylight before washing, before touching a switch.

Written purely out of love for the calm it offered for to calm someone else is calming, whether or not one can calm oneself.

If never delivered never so intended.

Her vocabulary refined by years of looking through the screen at the lilac that absorbed her witness.

So many contradictory measures taking up their positions.

The ubiquitous sense of scarcity especially where there was plenty.

So much turbulence in choosing.

She had to jimmy her way in.

Even an attempt to change her seating assignment.

All of her experience still looking for a language.

Honestly if she were able she would haul in one of the more animate clouds.

The following spring she promised herself to plant a white lilac.

She would take up her old position, hands folded, head back
waiting for the visions.

Like a Prisoner of Soft Words

We walk under the wires and the birds resettle.

We know where we're going but have not made up our mind

which way we will take to get there.

If we pass by the palmist's she can read our wayward lines.

We may drop things along the way that substantiate our having been here.

We will not be able to transmit any of these feelings verbatim.

By the time we reach the restaurant one of us is angry.

Here a door gives in to a courtyard

overlooking a ruined pool.

We touch the spot on our shirt where the ink has seeped.

The lonely outline of the host is discerned near an unlit sconce.

Something about an oar leaning against a wall.

As guests we are authorized not to notice.

We lack verisimilitude but we press on with intense resolve.

We are forced to admit we cannot reproduce the smell of the linden.

But we can tell you when we are standing

in the sphere of its fluency, its mystery, its heart-shaped leaves,

its special white honey, the precarious fabric of its protection.

The sound track isn't audible

when the wind picks up

we appear less posthumous against the silver exposures.

Like Having A Light At Your Back You Can't See But You Can Still Feel #1

As if it were streaming into your ear.

The edges of a room long vanished.

She is not really hearing what he's really saying.

The shine is going out of the ground
but they are sure of their footing.

It's not that they have been here before, but
they are young and they have water.

There are masses of rose hips and they are noisy.

The forward direction requires almost no effort.

Consonant with this feeling of harmony
comes another, less comfortable.

Not of being lost but of not belonging.

Yet they were not covering the air
with false words.

They moved along without talking,
not touching.

They wore their own smell.

She tastes salt and they must be getting closer.

Others are out there who are drifting.

If this took place anywhere near the presidential palace

It would be non-stop terrifying.

And this could be the reason she has started to scream.

LIKE THE SUN DOWN THERE

Early in the day they were driving past the small vineyard

They were looking forward to walking around in another town

They could find a wrought iron bench in a garden of splashy flowers

They might find a swimming hole

Just beyond the vineyard they passed a dog standing against the body of a dog

They passed a number of one-story houses sprouting rebar from the rooftops

A man balancing bundles on his handlebars

Plastic bags caught in organ cactus

The town was twisted and steep

The streets cobbled and shops full of punched tin

They sat on a wall and watched children play in the dust

At the waterworks women were washing mounds of colored clothing

A man walking his hog by a string knocked on a door in a wall and was let in

They walked down some steps into a candlelit room

The closeness the warmth the voices of people eating together

The sound of plates slowly being stacked and a bird in the kitchen

The disconsolate strain of a traditional song

The full and weary ride home

Just before the vineyard

The lights of the car picked out the standing dog, the form of the other one

Like Hearing Your Name Called in a Language You Don't Understand

Since the day the bell was cast

I have sat in the bishop's carved chair and waited my turn

with my feet crossed at the ankles, and the leather of my huaraches

cutting into the hide of my foot

From where I was sitting I watched the light being drawn off

the magnolias in the Plaza de Armas

while the voices of the others choired an evening

I have risen to the lectern when the eyes of the host summoned

I faced the great open doors as the faces of strangers
acknowledged their own losses

I saw the white trousers of the vendor flapping in the dust

His body engulfed in balloons

The children selling Chiclets dispersed

The shoe shine boy putting away his brushes, the sum of his inheritance

I have read what was written there, said Gracias and sat down again

I have climbed the pyramidal steps and felt winded and humbled

I have stood small and borracho and been glad
of not being thrown down the barranca alongside the pariah consul
in the celebrated book

In every sense have I felt lonelier than a clod of clay, a whip, a bolsa,
a skull of chocolate

though I have worn the medal of the old town with forlorn pleasure
I say unto you,

Comrades, be not in mourning for your being

to express happiness and expel scorpions is the best job on earth

LIKE THE GHOST OF A CARRIER PIGEON

In a couple of hours darkness will throw its blanket
over the scene   she will pretend to read a mystery
                    the mower and hammering will cease

The bees leave the andromeda and then

So much has been spent constructing a plausible life
she did not hear the engines of dissent run down

Some still attempt to cover the skull with the wire of their hair
                    others shave everything instead

A solitary relives the pleasure of releasing his bird

There is no sacrosanct version   there is only time

Even now   if someone yells Avalanche   she has one
thoughts shudder against the ribs and go still

Soon the son would be out running around in her car
with a sore throat   soon the decibels commence killing off hair cells

She checks to see if the phone is charged and then

The ones responsible for slaying the dreamer are mostly in the ground
but the ones responsible for slaying the dream

Suffer only metabolic syndrome

Even now   that her supply of contact lenses has dwindled
                    she was refusing to sing the Wal-Mart song

The bees would be back and then

All efforts at reconciliation aside   even if everyone exchanged germs
                    happiness is only for amateurs

A dress worn only once before has been hung on the door
                    the mirror under the cloth receives its image

Like Something in His Handwriting

It was hotter back then

No it wasn't it had to be cooler, clouded

A park down below where no one ever met

But men were pulled by dogs along paths made
by the walkers

And a nameless river through a photograph of woods

proposed a non-local reality

that shimmered at the instant of its own disappearance

She bought it, brought it back, propped it against

drywall where someone had penciled a message

The end of another summer wandered across yards
that weren't fenced or watered

If it rained, it rained

and then the rain inebriated us

A yellow leaf floated toward ground

transmitting a spot of optimism

through a slow intensification of color in the lower corner of the morning

Like Having A Light At Your Back You Can't See But You Can Still Feel #2

As if it were streaming into your ear.

The edges of a room long vanished.

She is not really hearing what he's really saying.

The shine is going out of the ground
but they are sure of their footing.

They have been here a thousand and one times.

There are masses of rose hips and they are noisy.

The forward direction requires almost no effort.

Consonant with this feeling of harmony
comes another, less comfortable.

Not of being lost but of not belonging.

Yet they were not covering the space
with false words.

They moved along without talking,
not touching.

They wore their own smell. The air
was salty.

Others were out there who were drifting.

It is a bay in New England.
closed to shell fishing after heavy rains.

The house is not far from here. Next to the old
burial ground.

Most nights aren't dark enough to see stars.

If a bad movie, a bad movie. If a bad meal,
a bad meal. If bad wine. Bad wine.

They read. And go to bed early. He puts on an eyemask.

She wants a light on. She wants to read.

No, he says, Turn it off.

Let me finish the chapter.

Turn it off, C.

The page then, she says. You have your mask on.

I can still feel it, he says, I can feel it

streaming in my ear. Besides,

he is adamant,

You just go to sleep at night

I go on a journey.

Like the Hour of Our Perfection

Whereas before things were all immanence,
Now were they all valence

In the breathing world where we met

Who presented initial shyness

Who disheveled the light at the threshold

With a look of near-adolescence, so one did not know
if he also slept with the men

And the ledge of a hip when

seen first from behind, a voice, an outline

And the breast spared after an early scare

Her amulet of dead rosesuckers

Her black hollyhocks soaring to the second story

His lemons cut into eight precise slices

A door hung by which one could leave if one chose to go

Always movement, hypotheticals, another qualm

The dashes of footprints after a shower

I'm not saying it did happen

I'm saying it could have it could have happened like this

Like something of ivory so scarce
and procured with such violence

What fell as a fine rug receives an harp

RE: HAPPINESS, IN PURSUIT THEREOF

It is 2005, just before landfall.
Here I am, a labyrinth, and I am a mess.
I am located at the corner of Waterway
and Bluff. I need your help. You will find me
to the left of the graveyard, where the trees
grow especially talkative at night,
where fog and alcohol rub off the edge.
We burn to make one another sing;
to stay the lake that it not boil, earth
not rock. We are running on Aztec time,
fifth and final cycle. Eyes switch on/off.
We would be mercurochrome to one another
bee balm or chamomile. We should be concrete,
glass and spandex. We should be digital, or
at least, early. Be ivory-billed. Invisible
except to the most prepared observer.
We will be stardust. Ancient tailings
of nothing. Elapsed breath. No,
we must first be ice. Be nails. Be teeth.
                              Be lightning.

NOTES ON THE POEMS

A Farm Boy

Warren J. Wright interviewed his father Ernie Edward Wright in December 1998 and most of the details were taken from that recorded memento and given form by his daughter Carolyn D. Wright on the occasion of his 90th birthday.

Just Whistle

Lines from the first stanza of Gerard Manley Hopkins's "No worst, there is none" are buried between words on the page beginning *No. It Worst. Destroys.* I have always revered the Hopkins poem, and feel a little perverse for the use to which I've put it. Even more so for borrowing descriptive terms of the teeming botanical aftermath of the bombing of Japan from John Hersey's shattering book *Hiroshima*. I was well aware then as I am now that a personal psychic and physical crisis is not like unto the cataclysm of war.

INDEX